Yugoslavia
After Tito

Westview Special Studies on the Soviet Union and Eastern Europe

Yugoslavia After Tito:
Scenarios and Implications
Gavriel D. Ra'anan

This study examines policy options, both for the USSR and the West, for the period after Marshal Josip Broz Tito passes from the scene. Proceeding on the assumption that Yugoslavia's future is of European, indeed global, significance, Gavriel Ra'anan considers various scenarios of a succession crisis. His point of departure is that the activist role in the region is most likely to be maintained by the Soviet Union, while the West, even if it does recognize that it has to play a significant part, well may restrict itself to an essentially reactive role. In this context, Ra'anan examines the military and political capabilities of the potential contestants and the constraints circumscribing their actions; he pays particular attention to the implications for NATO's southern flank of any reabsorption of Yugoslavia into the Soviet bloc. This study refrains from engaging in excessive speculation regarding individual contenders for Tito's inheritance, and devotes its analysis to the probable behavior of governments and other political group actors on the international and Yugoslav domestic scenes.

Gavriel D. Ra'anan is completing his graduate work in international relations, security studies, and international law at the Fletcher School of Law and Diplomacy. At Brown University, where he graduated with honors in international relations, he was editor-in-chief of the *Journal of the John Hay Society for Foreign Affairs.*

Yugoslavia After Tito

Scenarios and Implications

Gavriel D. Ra'anan

Westview Press • Boulder, Colorado

Westview Special Studies on the Soviet Union and Eastern Europe

Copyright © 1977 by Westview Press, Inc.

Published in 1977 in the United States of America by
  Westview Press, Inc.
  1898 Flatiron Court
  Boulder, Colorado 80301
  Frederick A. Praeger, Publisher and Editorial Director

Library of Congress Cataloging in Publication Data
Ra'anan, Gavriel D
  Yugoslavia after Tito.
  (Westview special studies on the Soviet Union and
Eastern Europe)
  Bibliography: p.
  1. Yugoslavia—Politics and government—1945-
2. Yugoslavia—Foreign relations—1945-   I. Title.
II. Series.
DR370.R25   320.9'497'02   77-4164
ISBN 0-89158-335-1

Printed and bound in the United States of America

To my parents,
who lovingly cajoled me into finishing this book.

Contents

Preface

This study attempts to examine policy options, both for the Soviet and Western camps, during the period after Marshal Josip Broz Tito passes from the scene. It proceeds on the assumption that Yugoslavia's future is of European—indeed, global—significance and evaluates the incentives of either camp to incur serious costs in taking steps that could determine that future. The book considers various scenarios of a succession crisis; however, it assumes that the activist role in the region is likely to be maintained by the Soviet Union, whereas the West—if, indeed, it recognizes that it has to play a significant part—well may restrict itself to an essentially reactive role.

In examining the military and political capabilities of the potential contestants and the constraints on their actions, this work pays particular attention to the implications for NATO's southern flank of a potential reabsorption of Yugoslavia into the Soviet bloc. I have refrained from speculating about individual contenders for Tito's inheritance, but, rather, devoted my analysis to the probable behavior of governments and other political "actors" on the international and Yugoslav domestic scenes.

While gathering documentation for this book, I was fortunate to obtain interviews with a number of experts who extended to me valuable assistance and guidance. Though in some instances I have acknowledged their contributions elsewhere in this study, this has not been possible in many cases. I wish to take this opportunity, therefore, to express my appreciation and gratitude in particular to the following personalities:

Admiral Stansfield Turner, former commander in chief of Allied Forces in Southern Europe, who graciously briefed me himself, offered his hospitality at his beautiful home in Naples, and granted me access to his staff of experts;

General George J. Keegan, Jr., former assistant chief of staff for intelligence, U.S. Air Force, who gave generously of his valuable time and insights;

Mr. John H. Morse, former deputy assistant secretary of defense for European and NATO affairs, who was most kind in arranging for me the briefings without which much of this work could not have been completed;

Mr. Alfred Vigderman, former foreign service officer and expert on Greek-Turkish-Cypriot affairs, who was most helpful not only in supplying illuminating information, but in making possible other important conversations here and abroad;

Admiral Julien Lebourgeois, former commander of the U.S. Naval War College, who kindly arranged key meetings overseas;

Captain James Patton (USN) of the policy planning staff, U.S. Department of State, who gave unsparingly of his time in discussing with me significant aspects of this study and in making possible other important meetings;

Major Roy W. Stafford (USAF), Office of the Defense Advisor, U.S. Mission, NATO Headquarters, Brussels, who was most helpful in arranging valuable appointments in Brussels and who, together with Mrs. Stafford, extended to me gracious hospitality;

Professor Dr. Ernst Kux, East European expert of the *Neue Zürcher Zeitung,* whose fresh insights into the situation proved invaluable;

Dr. and Mrs. Pan Vandoros, whose gracious hospitality and helpful contacts in Athens were much appreciated;

Brigadier Kenneth Hunt, of the International Institute of Strategic Studies, London, who assisted me in my work.

Last, but by no means least, I wish to thank the International Security Studies Program of the Fletcher School of Law and Diplomacy—in particular my faculty advisers, Professors Robert L. Pfaltzgraff, Jr., and Geoffrey Kemp, who made possible the travel grant which enabled me to do essential portions of this work in Europe and who have guided me in my graduate studies. I appreciate particularly my brother Michael's painstaking work in compiling the index of this book.

Needless to say, all the opinions expressed in this study, as well as any errors, are mine alone.

Gavriel D. Ra'anan
Medford, Massachusetts, 1977

Introduction

Yugoslavia is perhaps the most precarious entity in Eastern Europe. It consists of six "Socialist Republics" (Slovenia, Croatia, Bosnia-Hercegovina, Montenegro, Serbia, and Macedonia) and two "Autonomous Provinces" (Kosovo-Metohija or Kosmet, and the Vojvodina). It contains six different official "nationalities" (Serbs, Croats, Moslems, Slovenes, Macedonians, and Montenegrins) and two "national minorities" with one-half million or more members each (Albanians and Hungarians), as well as three different religions (Catholicism, Orthodoxy of various denominations, and Islam). Furthermore, the geographical distribution of the nationalities and minorities does not coincide with the territorial limits of the "Socialist Republics" and "Autonomous Provinces" (see Appendix 1). In the 1971 census, only 1 percent of the population described itself as "Yugoslav" without further elaboration. To some extent, the Yugoslav state originated as the artificial creation of the victors of World War I.

Even if the national groups were living in harmony with one another, the Yugoslav system would not be free from stresses and dangers. Yugoslavia has several neighbors staking irredentist claims upon its territory; Bulgaria and Albania have been asserting their demands concerning Macedonia and the Kosmet respectively, while Hungary and perhaps even Italy might, under suitable circumstances, resume advancing their claims respectively to the Vojvodina and to portions of Venezia-Giulia ceded to Yugoslavia by Italy after World War II. Moreover, the Yugoslav state shares common boundaries with Hungary and Bulgaria, two fairly loyal Warsaw Pact states. These countries might be used as bases of attack against Yugoslavia by Pact forces, led by the Soviet Union, should Moscow ever attempt to eradicate the renegade Yugoslav state, with which it has had intermittent difficulties for nearly three decades. Recognizing the dangers inherent in this situation, the framers of the 1976 National Democratic Party Platform made specific and blunt reference to the importance of maintaining Yugoslavia as a non-Soviet-dominated entity in Eastern Europe:

> The continued U.S.S.R. military dominance of many Eastern European countries remains a source of oppression for the peoples of those nations, an oppression we do not accept and to which we are morally opposed. Any attempt by the Soviet Union similarly to dominate other parts of Europe—such as Yugoslavia—would be an action posing a grave threat to peace.[1]

Unfortunately, the Yugoslav leadership does not have even a secure domestic base from which to defend itself. There is a longstanding tradition of Serbo-Croat animosity, dating back at least to the interwar era, during which the Serbs *de facto* ruled Yugoslavia from Belgrade. This period was followed immediately by an even less harmonious episode during World War II, when, after Hitler's dismemberment of Yugoslavia in

1941, Croatian fascists, called the Ustashi, massacred Serbs in the areas controlled by the newly created Croat State. The Ustashi were successfully combatted by Josip Broz Tito (although himself half-Croat) and his group of Partisans, which was composed to a considerable extent of ethnic Serbs from Croatia and of Montenegrins. Thus, Communism was viewed by many Croats as a substantially Serb phenomenon. The Albanian and Hungarian minorities, to a great extent, collaborated with the Italian and Hungarian occupation forces, and remained hostile to the Communists after the war ended. Thus, these groups were treated as potentially subversive elements after Tito took over Yugoslavia. Macedonians, many of whom regarded themselves as Bulgars and cooperated with Bulgarian occupation forces, 1941-44, finally were accorded the status of a separate "new" nationality after the war, having been compelled to pretend that they were mere "southern Serbs" from 1913 to 1941. However, the Macedonians resent having been prevented from realizing their original goal—reunification of the Bulgarian, Yugoslav, and Greek portions of Macedonia—and having been denied full and genuine autonomy.[2] More recent conflicts have seen the economically developed Slovene and Croat Socialist Republics of northern Yugoslavia allied against a southern coalition of Serbia, the underdeveloped Socialist Republics (Bosnia, Montenegro, and Macedonia), and the Kosmet in disputes concerning economic and developmental policies.

On another level, the Yugoslav elite is divided over ideological questions concerning the proper implementation of "self-management socialism" and of liberalization of restrictions on freedom of expression. While recent developments have shown that the central bureaucracy is developing an increasingly rigid, antiliberal stance, the Croat, Serb, and Slovene intellectual communities, by contrast, have produced significant elements belonging to the so-called New Left, which advocates decentralization and expansion of civil liberties. Most notable among these groups has been the editorial board of the Zagreb journal *Praxis*.

This book examines the nexus between these various questions in an attempt to assess the potential difficulties confronting the Yugoslav state in the years ahead, particularly when the inevitable occurs and Tito passes from the scene. The viability of the Yugoslav state will be placed in the context of the NATO–Warsaw Pact strategic balance in the Mediterranean. In attempting to examine the implications of changes in Yugoslavia's present situation for the states in the region and for the two superpowers and their respective allies, this study will be divided into two sections.

The first part deals primarily with domestic problems besetting the Yugoslav state. The initial chapter considers irredentist claims that are advanced regarding certain areas of Yugoslavia and attempts to relate these demands to Yugoslavia's nationality problems. The second chapter is concerned with the long-standing grievances of the two developed republics, Croatia and Slovenia. The following chapter deals with the Belgrade regime's struggle against the New Left in Yugoslavia. The final chapter in the first part describes the structure of government designated for the post-Tito era, as well as the likely role of the army during the succession period.

The second part deals primarily with the international implications of a succession crisis. Chapter 5, with which that part of the book opens, explores Soviet attitudes toward Yugoslavia and their impact on that country. The following two chapters deal with the political, operational, and perceptual implications for countries in the regions affected by potential Soviet actions in Yugoslavia and with the military and strategic implications of such intervention for the two great military alliances in Europe. Chapter 8 considers the military position of Yugoslavia and assesses its ability to defend itself against foreign incursion under various circumstances. Chapter 9 examines concessions made to the Soviet leadership by Marshal Tito and evaluates the possible effects of anticipatory appeasement of the Kremlin. The final chapter reviews probable scenarios for the post-Tito period, analyzing policy options available to the USSR and the West under the most likely contingencies.

Part 1

Domestic Aspects

1
Irredentism and Policy

Yugoslavia's nationality problems are likely to tempt foreign interference or even intervention during the turmoil of a succession crisis. Yugoslavia is vulnerable since it includes within its boundaries several areas which, by virtue of the ethnic affinities of their inhabitants and their cultural and historic ties to Yugoslavia's neighbors, are the objects of irredentist claims by those neighbors. Thus Yugoslavia includes about half a million Hungarians (most of whom live in the Autonomous Province of Vojvodina), more than 1.3 million Albanians (nearly 1 million of whom live in the Autonomous Province of Kosovo-Metohija), and well over a million "Macedonians," who constitute slightly over 60 percent of the population of the Yugoslav (or Vardar) portion of Macedonia.[1] Of particular significance, in view of irredentist claims, is the rapid demographic growth of Yugoslavia's Albanians and, to a lesser degree, Macedonians. Whereas in 1961 the Albanians comprised 4.9 percent of the Yugoslav population, by 1971 they had risen to 6.4 percent of the population. The Macedonians, during the same period, enjoyed a more modest increase, rising from 5.6 percent to 5.8 percent of the country's inhabitants.[2]

The Macedonian problem is proverbially complex. Bulgaria, with some very brief exceptions, has persistently claimed that "Macedonians" are merely ethnolinguistic and cultural Bulgars who live in Macedonia, most of which was included in the First Bulgarian Empire, as early as the ninth century A.D.[3] Macedonia at present is divided between Bulgaria (the so-called Pirin region), Yugoslavia (the Vardar region), and Greece.

The Bulgars view the present situation as a continuation of the injustice perpetrated both by the 1878 Congress of Berlin and by the 1913 Treaty of Bucharest, which concluded the Second Balkan War (1912-13). They claim that in both cases power politics prevailed to deprive the Macedonians of their right to self-determination.[4] In fact, there is little question that, as late as the end of the nineteenth century, Macedonian literary and cultural initiatives were virtually indistinguishable from their Bulgarian counterparts.[5]

Following their 1913 annexation of Vardar Macedonia, the Serbs embarked upon a program of forced "Serbization"; accompanying that policy was severe persecution, which bore witness to the degree of "Bulgarophilism" still extant in the Serb-occupied portion of Macedonia.[6] Thus it appears that when the Bulgarians occupied Yugoslav Macedonia in 1941 they were greeted, in many instances, as liberating heroes. However, the Bulgarian occupation of Vardar Macedonia proved less than completely idyllic, and the Macedonians lost some of their enthusiasm for their Bulgarian brethren.[7]

Following World War II, the communists took over both Yugoslavia and Bulgaria. Already during the 1930s, the Yugoslav Communist Party (CPY), following a new Comintern "line," had begun to assert that there was an independent Macedonian nationality. The Bulgarian Communist Party, however, along with virtually all other parties in Bulgaria, still claimed that Macedonians were merely Bulgars.[8] However, in 1944 the Bulgarian Communist Party changed its position and until 1948 followed the same line as the CPY and the newly-founded Cominform, in agreeing that Macedonians were, in fact, a separate nationality and that Macedonia should be united and included as a single autonomous entity in a Balkan federation being planned at that time. The Bulgarian leaders assumed that Macedonia naturally would gravitate toward Bulgaria by virtue of the two areas' historic, cultural, and linguistic ties.[9] Thus Sofia viewed the unification and federation scheme as being very much in its own interest, since it would facilitate extending Bulgarian influence to the Yugoslav sector of Macedonia. The Yugoslavs, on the other hand, hoped that, since the plan would mean severing Pirin Macedonia from Bulgaria, it would reduce Bulgarian influence in the region as a whole.[10] So wholehearted became the Bulgarian dedication to this proposal that Sofia went so far as to assert that its own Macedonian population was culturally distinct from other Bulgars—and followed logically by making provisions for "compulsory" instruction in the "Macedonian" language, "compulsory" subscription to "Macedonian" language newspapers, and registration of Pirin Macedonians as members of the "Macedonian" nationality in the Bulgarian census.[11]

However, following the 1948 expulsion of Yugoslavia from the Cominform and the realization by Sofia that the proposed Balkan federation had been stillborn, the Bulgarian leadership began to revert to its pre-1944 line, claiming once again that Macedonians were Bulgars, and decrying the "Serbization" of Vardar Macedonia. Subsequent to the 1956 Bulgarian census, traces of a separate "Macedonian" nationality all but disappeared in Bulgaria; Pirin, which had registered some 166,000 "Macedonians" in 1946 and almost 188,000 members of that nationality in 1956, showed only 8,750 in the 1965 census.[12]

However, having given ammunition to the CPY on the Macedonian question by adopting, for a brief period, the Yugoslav position on the question of the existence of an independent "Macedonian" nationality, the Bulgarians had undermined their irredentist claims to the Vardar region. Moreover, as a result of this temporary deviation, Sofia paved the way for Yugoslavia to take the ideological offensive with claims both to Pirin and to Greek Macedonia, in the name of "Macedonian unification and self-determination."[13] The Yugoslavs subsequently even lodged complaints regarding the alleged "repression" of "Macedonians" in Bulgaria, and made enquiries as to the whereabouts of the 188,000 "Macedonians" who had been registered in Pirin in 1956.[14] Yugoslav claims to Greek Macedonia, however, were laid aside as part of the Yugoslav policy, after the break with Stalin, of achieving good relations with Greece, as with other pro-Western states—a policy symbolized by the 1949 closing of the Yugoslav border to Greek Communist guerrilla forces and by the signing of the 1953/54 Balkan Pacts between Greece, Turkey, and Yugoslavia.[15] However, the Macedonian question has continued to fester as a major impediment to better Yugoslav-Bulgarian relations, and polemics of varying degrees of intensity have poisoned the atmosphere between the two countries during the last quarter-century.

The polemics of recent years have concentrated primarily on two themes. First, the two Communist neighbors have argued strenuously about the role of the Bulgarian army in "liberating Macedonia" during 1944—a role which, of course, is denigrated by Belgrade and stressed by Sofia.[16] A second issue, of far greater importance, is the debate mentioned earlier regarding the treatment by the Yugoslav and Bulgarian governments of their respective Macedonian populations. This question is much more significant than the theoretical debate concerning the role of the Bulgarian army thirty years ago, since it has potentially serious implications for the internal security of the two states. Each side has claimed that the other has been culturally and economically repressing its "Macedonian" inhabitants.

Some of the key questions—the answers to which probably would determine the outcome of the Macedonian conflict—are:

- How much sentiment would there be within Vardar Macedonia for detachment of that region from Yugoslavia and for reunification with the rest of Macedonia under Bulgarian rule?
- How far would the Bulgarians be willing to go in attempting to realize their long-standing goal of obtaining a reversal of the post-1878 situation?
- How much support would the Bulgarians, who have dutifully followed the Soviet line since World War II, receive from the Soviet Union?

Prior to World War II there was no clear indication as to which solution would be preferred by the majority of Vardar Macedonians.[17] Certainly, there had been long-standing opposition to Serb domination of the Macedonians.[18] This had been fueled by intermittent cooperation between the Bulgars and Macedonian nationalists, most notable in the IMRO (Internal Macedonian Revolutionary Organization) during the 1930s.[19] However, opposition to Serb rule does not by itself indicate majority support either for incorporation into the Bulgarian state or for the creation of an independent Macedonia. It is true, though, that as early as the 1930s the Macedonian Communist Party included a significant segment dedicated to achieving a separate Macedonian political entity.[20]

Since 1945, Belgrade has engaged in an intense program of "nation-building" in Vardar Macedonia, going to the extreme of rewriting Macedonian history so as to expunge all traces of former connections with Bulgaria and present the past as a long historical process of alleged Macedonian independent development.[21] In addition, the Yugoslavs, in effect, have fabricated a Macedonian "literary language" in order to justify claims of a separate cultural tradition.[22] This language, which was taught throughout the Vardar in the 1950s, borrowed extensively both from Serbo-Croat and from Russian in an attempt to minimize the similarity between the languages spoken in Macedonia and Bulgaria.[23] Still another manifestation of the "Macedonization" policy of the Yugoslav government was the granting in 1967 of independent status to the Macedonian Orthodox Church, which previously had been operating under the aegis of the Serbian Orthodox Church. This element is very important, since religion and ethnicity always have been closely related in the Balkans.[24]

To some extent, the Yugoslav policy seems to have succeeded in de-Bulgarizing the Macedonian population of Yugoslavia. While at present there does not seem to be much, if any, truth to Yugoslav claims that a separate status is desired by Bulgaria's "Pirin Macedonians," there is also no evidence that "Vardar Macedonians" are seized by an overwhelming desire to rebel against Yugoslav rule.[25] Nevertheless, there are indications that some pro-Bulgar sentiment still exists in Yugoslav Macedonia. Specifically, the Yugoslav government has consistently listed "nationalist deviations" as one of the major problems encountered in Macedonia. Moreover, it has vehemently attacked Macedonians who have moved to Bulgaria and declared themselves to be Bulgars, a response which would seem to indicate feelings of considerable concern on the part of Belgrade. One such emigré who attracted a particularly large amount of adverse commentary was Venko Markovski, a former Yugoslav Macedonian who has since achieved renown as a Bulgarian poet.[26]

What, then, might Bulgarian reactions be to a Yugoslav

succession crisis? Certainly Sofia would be tempted to interfere to some degree, if not to intervene directly, on behalf of what it still considers to be members of its own ethnic family. However, it is inconceivable that the Bulgars would take direct action against the Yugoslavs without at least obtaining prior Soviet agreement, if not actual Soviet aid. While the intensity of Bulgarian polemics against Yugoslavia has not been always commensurate with the degree of Soviet-Yugoslav animosity, departure from the Soviet line on any issue has never been of sufficient magnitude to indicate Sofia's willingness to take such a major step by itself.[27] Moreover, it would be militarily unfeasible to do so (see Chapter 8). At most, the Bulgarians, on their own, might be prepared to incite disturbances in the Vardar region, with the remote possibility that these might culminate in an uprising.

A Soviet decision to intervene would depend on a number of criteria: how unfavorably Moscow viewed Tito's successor(s); its estimate of the Yugoslav will to resist and of the efficiency and loyalty of the Yugoslav army and the Territorial Defense Forces; its perceptions of the possible reactions of the United States, other NATO members, China, and the Romanians; and the degree of indigenous Macedonian support that could be generated for a move to bring about separation from Yugoslavia. Given the long history of Moscow's difficulties with Tito, as well as the recent fluctuations in Yugoslav-Soviet relations, the Soviet leaders well might be tempted either to dismember the Yugoslav state or to impose a docile successor regime in Belgrade. Certainly, the USSR would view with dislike and suspicion a Yugoslav successor regime purporting to be "Titoist," as Tito's heirs are very likely to be. A secession move in Macedonia might well afford "Cominformist" elements there and in Belgrade a perfect opportunity to take command. The recent "Cominformist" arrests in Yugoslavia would seem to indicate that the Soviet Union indeed is seeking to undermine the Titoist state and probably is attempting to establish a base there, in anticipation of Tito's demise.

A second major irredentist problem which could prove extremely troublesome for Yugoslavia is the Albanian issue. Most of the 1.3 million Albanians in Yugoslavia are concentrated in the Kosmet and in a portion of Macedonia immediately adjacent to Albania.[28] There areas, populated by over one-third of all the Albanians in the world, serve as the object of a serious irredentist claim by the Albanian state (the leadership of which still retains some degree of Chinese support). The Albanians in the Kosmet (by far the poorest region in Yugoslavia, averaging only 30 percent of Yugoslavia's overall per capita income) unquestionably are nationally conscious.[29] Periodically, they have resorted to various degrees of violence—at times apparently at the behest of the Albanian government and on other occasions spontaneously. The most notable uprising occurred in November 1968, when, following a long period of high-level Albanian incitement, the local populace engaged in large-scale rioting, calling for union of the Kosmet and Albania. Ironically, these demonstrations erupted at a time when, in the wake of the Soviet invasion of Czechoslovakia, the Albanians and Yugoslavs just had begun to effect a rapprochement of sorts.[30] Presumably, the brutal show of Soviet intolerance for Czech liberalization was taken most seriously by these two parties, which have good reason themselves to fear Soviet punishment for their own major ideological deviations. However, despite the relaxation of tensions between Yugoslavia and Albania after the invasion of Czechoslovakia, there have been, since that time, recurrences of tension and conflict in the Kosmet, most notably early in 1975.[31] Increased cooperation, trade, and cultural exchange between Albania and the Kosmet simply have not served to diffuse or obscure the grievances of Yugoslavia's Albanians, who claim to be victims of ethnic, religious (most Albanians in

Yugoslavia are practicing Moslems), and economic oppression.[32] (With respect to the last question, it is relevant to point out that between 1947 and 1972 the economic ratio between the Kosmet and the rest of Yugoslavia, in terms of gross product per capita, deteriorated from 4:7 in 1947 to about 2:7 in 1972. The Kosmet average dipped to a mere 28 percent of the Yugoslav average.)[33] The 1975 demonstrations placed such a strain on relations between the two countries that Yugoslavia apparently shelved its policy of seeking actively a closer relationship with Albania.[34] The earlier approach had been enunciated by Tito in two statements: "What unites the two countries is more important than what divides us" and "Yugoslavia and Albania are of enormous importance for stability in the Balkans."[35] He added that the two states should avoid disagreements which could prompt interference from abroad—an obvious reference to the threat posed to both by the USSR.[36]

Yugoslavia recently initiated a new propaganda campaign stressing the need to stamp out Albanian irredentism.[37] The year 1976 was a particularly difficult period for Belgrade-Tirana relations. Early in the year, thirty-one ethnic Albanians were imprisoned for having belonged allegedly to an underground "Albanian national liberation movement" advocating unification of Kosovo with Albania. This group was accused of receiving "instructions" from unspecified sources, and adopting political positions "based on dogmatic Stalinist ideology." Since Albania is the only avowedly Stalinist state in Europe, clearly the Yugoslav authorities were hinting that the Albanian government was involved in the irredentist conspiracy. Compounding the difficulties between the two states during 1976 was a border incident in which the captain of an Albanian fishing vessel was shot and killed by Yugoslav border guards, allegedly for having refused to obey orders while in Yugoslav territorial waters. As a result of this incident, and of the arrests of ethnic Albanians in Yugoslavia, the Albanian government stepped up its denunciations of the Belgrade regime.[38] Friction between the two states, along with increasing unrest within Kosovo, probably would encourage the Soviet Union to intervene in Yugoslavia, if these difficulties persisted after Tito's demise.

Thus, Kosovo is an area fraught with potential dangers which well might rise to the surface during a Yugoslav succession crisis. A key element in such a situation would be the status of Albania in the context of the Sino-Soviet rift. For some time now, the Soviet Union has been attempting to woo the Albanians away from the Chinese and back into the Soviet bloc. At the same time, the Soviet leaders have been attempting a rapprochement with Yugoslavia.[39] It is possible that the Soviet Union might dangle the bait of annexation of the Kosmet before the Albanians, in the event of a Yugoslav succession crisis, hoping to detach them from China once and for all. That the Chinese, by their own admission, could exert little leverage on events in a region so distant from them was indicated by Chou En-lai's statement, "A fire cannot be extinguished with water from a distant well."[40] Thus probably Peking could not compete with effective counteroffers. However, the Albanians have not responded favorably to Soviet overtures—as was demonstrated by Premier Enver Hoxha's declaration, "Not being able to bite our hand, the Soviet revisionists now want to kiss it."[41] Perhaps even more significant has been Albanian criticism of Soviet foreign policy, including Tirana's cheers from the sidelines for apparent Soviet setbacks in the Middle East.[42] No doubt equally irritating to the USSR has been Albanian criticism of Soviet domination of the Eastern European satellite states. An editorial signed by Ramiz Alija (a member of the Albanian Politburo and of the Secretariat of the Albanian Workers' Party) in the November 16, 1975, edition of the journal *Zeri i Popullit* asserted that the peoples of the satellite countries suffered under the double oppression of rule by "local revisionist cliques" and the "yoke of Soviet social imperialism." As indicated by the harsh Soviet reactions to Hungarian and Czechoslovak attempts to gain a measure of independence, this is an issue about which the Kremlin feels most sensitive. The Belgrade government—perhaps because Yugoslavia, unlike Albania, borders on Warsaw Pact territory—has been considerably more circumspect in dealing with the subject of the Soviet relationship with its client states.[43]

Despite recent difficulties between the two states, Albania generally has shown itself to be more responsive to Yugoslav overtures, since 1968, than to Soviet initiatives. Certainly, the warm Yugoslav statements concerning Albania, during the period following the Soviet march into Prague and the proclamation of the Brezhnev Doctrine, would seem to indicate that a genuine improvement did occur in relations between Belgrade and Tirana, based on the necessity of presenting a united front against Soviet intervention. Typical of Belgrade's statements during this period, which lasted well into 1975, was the following comment by Tito:

> Yugoslavia and Albania are of enormous importance for stability in the Balkans. Should Yugoslavia and Albania indulge in disagreement, many would try to interfere. Our mutual interests are so great—and I believe that the Albanian leaders also see this—that we shall develop our relations to our mutual benefit.[44]

During recent years, economic and cultural relations and tourism between the two countries were restored, as were diplomatic relations at the ambassadorial level. At the same time, there was a clear diminution of shrill polemics regarding the Kosovo.[45] These diatribes, however, were stepped up again in the fall of 1975.

While attempting to achieve a rapprochement with Albania, Yugoslavia began improving its relations with Mao's China. This development, which is still continuing, was illustrated in 1975 by the visit to China of the late Yugoslav prime minister, Bijedic. While in Peking, Bijedic made a point of repeating Mao's slogan, "Dig tunnels, store wheat, never try to practice hegemonism"—a clear reference to the mutual interests of the two governments in joining hands to oppose Soviet imperialism.[46]

There are several sound reasons why the Albanian leadership might have second thoughts should an opportunity actually occur for annexing the Kosmet. While Albanian irredentism has served as a significant issue upon which to focus national attention and to divert domestic discontent, Kosovo might become a liability for Tirana if it were actually incorporated into Albania. The people of the region have rioted against the Yugoslav government to protest alleged religious suppression (e.g., of Islamic instruction)—an issue which could well come to the fore again were the Kosmet to be incorporated into Albania, "the world's first atheistic state."[47] Moreover, quite apart from the problems posed by its devout Moslem masses, Kosovo has its own secular Albanian (Communist) leadership, which might not relish relinquishing status and authority to Tirana. Furthermore, Yugoslavia at present serves as a useful buffer between Albania and the Soviet Union; regardless of its feelings toward the Serbs, Tirana would have to think long and hard before embarking on a policy which would contribute to the dissolution of that buffer. In addition, Kosovo contains approximately 300,000 non-Albanians, including almost 250,000 Serbs.[48] These minorities would constitute an alien entity comprising nearly 10 percent of the total population of a potential Albanian-Kosmet confederation. It is improbable that the Albanian leadership would be very enthusiastic at the prospect of importing a serious minority problem into the ethnically homogeneous Albanian state, particularly since the generally more advanced Serbs would hardly "assimilate downward" to the Albanian level. Equally problematic for Tirana might be any attempt to implement a mass expulsion of Serbs from the Kosmet.

Given their military inferiority, it is unlikely that the Albanians could succeed in forcibly annexing the Kosmet (even if they enjoyed indigenous support) unless such a campaign were to be coordinated with the Soviet Union. It would appear that any benefits to be derived from obtaining the Kosmet might be outweighed by the danger of losing Albanian sovereignty itself to Soviet domination in such an event. However, if the Albanians were to view that sovereignty as being in severe jeopardy anyway, they might have no choice but to cooperate with the increasingly preponderant power of the USSR in the Mediterranean.

As vitriolic a form as Albanian-Soviet polemics may have assumed throughout the 1960s and the first half of the 1970s, it must be recalled that Yugoslav-Albanian mutual recriminations by far antedate those between Tirana and Moscow. During the immediate post–World War II period, the present Albanian party leader, Enver Hoxha, headed a faction which was opposed by a Belgrade-backed group led by Koci Xoxe. In 1945-48, during which time Tito was in the good graces of Moscow, Albania was treated as an unofficial puppet state of Yugoslavia and as such was not even represented at the founding meeting of the Cominform.[49] Moreover, Albania in this period received economic aid not directly from Moscow but rather through Belgrade, although Yugoslavia itself was incapable of supplying much investment capital to Tirana. According to Milovan Djilas, Stalin (whether seriously or in jest) told the Yugoslav leader in January 1948 that he favored Yugoslavia "swallowing" Albania. Possibly only the Moscow-

Belgrade rupture in 1948 saved the autonomy of Albania (and, perhaps more significantly, the lives of the anti-Belgrade Albanian faction led by Hoxha). Throughout the 1950s, Albania continued to remonstrate against Tito. After Khrushchev initiated his rapprochement with Tito in 1955, domestic Albanian factions opposed to Hoxha apparently received encouragement—Hoxha was identified clearly as anti-Yugoslav; consequently, his standing was jeopardized by Tito's success. However, the opposition to Hoxha was ruthlessly purged in Tirana. As the Sino-Soviet rift developed during the late 1950s, the issue of the Soviet rapprochement with Yugoslavia became a focal point in Chinese opposition to the Soviet leadership.[50]

Peking's posture regarding the Moscow-Belgrade rapprochement probably was no more than a symbol of the comprehensive (anti-Soviet) militant line adopted by Mao as he switched from the moderate "Hundred Flowers" policy of 1957 to the radicalism of the Great Leap Forward of 1959 (and as the unwillingness of Moscow to aid the PRC in its activist foreign policy vis-à-vis Taiwan began to annoy Mao). Albanian opposition to improving relations with Tito clearly stemmed from Enver Hoxha's personal fear and dislike of the Yugoslav leaders, who nearly cost him his position and conceivably endangered his life. The Chinese-Albanian alliance was not surprising, since both parties had good reasons to oppose the Khrushchev-Tito flirtation. However, it may be stated with some justification that, while Hoxha in recent years pursued a "left wing" line largely because he opposed Tito—and thus also "Titoism" (which, after 1948, ceased being "leftist" and came to be viewed as a "rightist" national deviation)—Mao had to oppose Tito because the Chinese leadership had adopted a left-wing policy. Thus, while Mao's anti-Tito policy (and, hence, his alliance with Albania) was a by-product of his ideological pursuits, Hoxha's shift from Moscow to Peking was a by-product of his basic policy—namely, opposition to Yugoslavia. Should Moscow radically alter its policy of accommodation with Titoism and invade Yugoslavia, Hoxha, assuming that he is still in power, would be deprived of his major reason for opposing the Kremlin: namely, Russia's erstwhile flirtation with Tito. Consequently, the Albanian leader conceivably might reverse his policy in such a contingency and decide to cooperate with the Soviet Union. In fact, since the death of Mao, the Albanian leadership does appear to have been disengaging from its Chinese connections.[51] If, indeed, this is the case, it is just possible that Albania might move back toward the USSR.

Whether or not such a contingency is within the realm of feasibility, given Hoxha's deep emotional investment in achieving freedom from Soviet shackles, it is by no means certain that, if and when a succession crisis in Yugoslavia occurs, the current Albanian regime still will be in power. First of all, Hoxha, the leading member of the triumvirate, while not nearly as old as Tito, is sixty-nine; second, it is possible that four consecutive years of purges are indicative of dissatisfaction within the Albanian state. That country, which has the lowest standard of living in Europe, probably could improve its financial lot if it were to reestablish normal relations with the Soviet Union or initiate links with the West. If a new Tirana leadership were to emerge, therefore, it might perceive incentives for shifting Albanian foreign policy away from the existing line of isolation from all states but China.[52]

It is interesting that Albania has adopted constitutional provisions imitating two that were included in the 1974 Yugoslav constitution. One of these articles forbids anyone "to sign or accept in the name of the Peoples' Socialist Republic of Albania a capitulation or occupation of the country." Such an act is condemned as treason (article 93). The following article (94) prohibits "the stationing of foreign military bases and

troops on the territory of the People's Socialist Republic of
Albania."[53] It would appear that the Tirana government, like
its counterpart in Belgrade, is concerned with the possibility
that a faction within the party might request Soviet aid. Since a
new leadership which managed to regain the Kosmet, even if it
were to make great concessions to the USSR, would likely be
perceived as a legitimate nationalist force, Tirana's and Belgrade's concerns appear warranted, viewed in the context of
possible Soviet designs with respect to Yugoslavia.

Unlike the Macedonians and Albanians in Yugoslavia, the
Hungarian (Magyar) minority in the Vojvodina has not been
the object (since the Cominform period) of major pressures
from Belgrade or serious incitement by the Budapest government. The Yugoslavs have gone out of their way to assure the
Hungarian leadership that general harmony prevails in the
Vojvodina. This is demonstrated by the following statement
emanating from a Magyar Central Committee member of the
League of Communists of Croatia (in connection with the visit
of the Hungarian foreign minister, Frigyes Puja, to Yugoslavia in January 1975):

In some countries members of national minorities are
considered second class citizens; in others efforts have
been made to assimilate national minorities at any cost;
the right to use their own language, national designation,
and culture is denied. But Yugoslavia has demonstrated
how national minorities should be treated, and began to
do so even during the struggle for national liberation. And
the situation has improved as our state has developed.[54]

He went on to add that "almost all Hungarian children in
Yugoslavia acquire their first knowledge in their mother
tongue."[55]

Hungarian-Yugoslav relations have been harmonious to the

point that the Yugoslavs have allowed Vojvodina Hungarians to attend medical school in Hungary.[56] Any serious conflict between the two states over the Vojvodina at this time would appear to be improbable. A major change in the Hungarian-Yugoslav frontier would pose grave problems, in view of the fact that (unlike the Albanians, who constitute an overwhelming majority of the Kosmet's inhabitants) Hungarians now are in a distinct minority in the Vojvodina, where Serbs outnumber them five to two.[57] However, Hungary might well become embroiled in a conflict with Yugoslavia in the context of a Soviet-led Warsaw Pact attack upon the latter, along the lines of the 1968 invasion of Czechoslovakia. This possibility will be discussed in detail subsequently. In such an eventuality, raising the issue of the Hungarian minority in the Vojvodina might provide both the pretext for an attack and an inducement or reward for Hungarian participation in an invasion of Yugoslavia (i.e., by holding out the prospect of regaining parts of the Vojvodina).

It has been suggested that the Soviet insistence upon exclusion of Hungary from the list of states to be considered in the MBFR (Mutual and Balanced Force Reduction) negotiations was based at least in part upon the desire of the Soviet Union to maintain a significant Warsaw Pact military force along the northern border of Yugoslavia.[58] Certainly this armed presence provides the Soviet Union with a base for invasion or less overt forms of interference in the affairs of the Yugoslav state. The large-scale presence of the Red Army in Hungary, moreover, cannot but enhance the credibility of factions in Yugoslavia advocating a pro-Moscow line. It might be assumed also that the Soviet presence on Hungarian territory guarantees that Budapest will commit troops to an invasion of Yugoslavia, if Moscow should decide to opt for such a policy. In this connection, it should be pointed out that, despite likely residual Hungarian bitterness over the events of 1956, Hungarian troops in fact did participate in the 1968 Warsaw Pact elimination of the "liberal" Dubček regime. Part of the Soviet incentive for including Hungarian forces among the invaders was reported to have been the presence of some 650,000 ethnic Hungarians in Slovakia—a situation analogous to that in Yugoslavia, where a large Hungarian minority inhabits the Vojvodina region of northern Serbia.[59] The 1968 precedent actually does not bode well for the USSR if it hopes to see ethnic Hungarians in Yugoslavia welcome Hungarian soldiers as liberators from the yoke of Serb oppression. Apparently, in 1968 the Hungarian army was greeted as anything but liberators: in fact, Hungarian army officers had to ban fraternization between Hungarian troops and local ethnic Hungarians, who tried to convince the invading soldiers to accept the merits of a Dubčekist line. However, what in social scientific parlance is referred to as the "specific situational variables" may be different in Yugoslavia, and it is possible that Hungarian troops would be better received by ethnic Hungarians in that country.

There have been border disputes between Italy and Yugoslavia, particularly in the Trieste area, and recent relations have been less than ideal.[60] However, there is no sizable Italian minority left in Yugoslavia; consequently Italians lack motivations that provide fertile soil for Bulgarian, Albanian, or even Hungarian irredentism.[61] Moreover, an armed conflict with a Communist country, even though it be a renegade from the bloc, would be fraught with sufficient potential danger to preclude any thought of Italian intervention in Yugoslavia. A provocative question is how these considerations might be affected by the rise to power of the PCI—a contingency that cannot be ruled out after the 1975 local and 1976 national elections in Italy. Paradoxically, a Communist-ruled Italy might be inclined to renew the attempt to redress Italian grievances against Yugoslavia in the Trieste hinterland and in Istria (see Chapter 6).

2
Grievances and Ethnic Conflicts

The history of Serbo-Croat relations within the Yugoslav state is hardly a tale of amicable coexistence between ethnolinguistic kinsmen. The two peoples are virtually identical, except for religious affiliation (the Serbs being Orthodox and the Croats Roman Catholic), script (the Serbs employ the Cyrillic script, while the Croats use the Latin alphabet), and minor variations of pronunciation; however, there is a long history of disharmony and strife between the two peoples—conflict which has not abated substantially under Yugoslav socialism.

Late in 1971, Croatian discontent with what was felt to be a continuation of the Serb domination of Yugoslavia that started in 1918 boiled over. Tito responded to unrest in Croatia with a mass purge of officials of the Croatian Communist Party. Subsequently there were purges of Croat intellectuals and restrictions were placed upon Croatian cultural organizations and mass media. Purges on a smaller scale were directed at nationalist elements among the Communist elite of other socialist republics.

Causes of the strife in 1971 are numerous and rather difficult to pinpoint. Certainly, traditional antipathies have not disappeared; if anything, they seem to have taken on new dimensions. According to one source, Croats tend to accuse Serbs, collectively, of having Muskovite leanings; equally inaccurate Serb claims may be heard that most Croats have never fully repudiated the Ustasha past and thus have "fascist" leanings. Furthermore, Serbs have been known to assert that Croats, as a group, would like to "sell out" to the West.[1]

Another theory regarding the 1971 Croat nationalist outburst was propounded by the anti-nationalist professor Stipe Suvar. He described the phenomenon as inherent in the development of Communist states, since communism, in its early stages, deprives the individual of *die Gemeinschaft* (the community) without, as yet, successfully promoting the arrival of its replacement, *die Gesellschaft* (society). This is claimed to be particularly relevant in view of the inability of the state to realize what have become exaggerated utopian goals.[2]

Specific claims made by Croats (and, to a lesser degree, by Slovenes) regarding Serb suppression of other nationalities refer to Serb domination of the army (see Chapter 8), increasing limitations placed on religious freedom of non-Orthodox denominations, particularly Catholics (in the name of separation of church and state), and economic exploitation of the highly developed republics of Slovenia and Croatia.

Claims concerning restrictions upon the religious activities of Catholics and Moslems, particularly in the Kosovo, have been conceded by the central government to be essentially accurate. However, such interference is explained officially as constituting a reaction to the far higher levels of activism and of nationalist sentiment within Catholic and Moslem religious organizations than are apparent within Orthodox groups.[3] While some restrictions have been placed also upon the Orthodox church, these are not associated with the nationality problem and thus constitute a somewhat less sensitive issue than does Belgrade's pressure on other religious groups. Nevertheless, if intensified, limitations upon Orthodox believers too could give rise to serious problems.[4]

In January 1971 the Croatian National Assembly attempted to compensate for the alleged pro-Serb slant of the Yugoslav army by passing the "law on nationwide defense of the socialist republic of Croatia," which created the first Territorial Defense unit in Yugoslavia.[5] While this aspect of the legislation was sanctioned by the federal government, which encouraged the formation of such units throughout the country, the bill contained intentionally ambiguous definitions of the intended functions of the force—a fact which must have caused concern in Belgrade. Specifically, the Croat assembly defined the territorial force as responsible for the "sovereignty, constitutional order, inviolability and wholeness of the [Croat] territory."[6] Perhaps even more objectionable from Belgrade's point of view was the ambiguity of the 1971 law in defining the potential enemies against whom Croatian sovereignty had to be protected. The Croats simply did not word the text in a manner that would preclude the defense of their republic's sovereignty against intrusions by the Yugoslav central government and its armed services. This concept of the sovereignty of Croatia, as reiterated in several sections of the Croatian constitution, was unacceptable to the Yugoslav central government—a view made clear by Tito in a statement to the effect that real sovereignty could be enjoyed only by Yugoslavia as a whole.[7] The complete decentralization of the Yugoslav forces implied by the Croatian law was entirely unacceptable to Tito, of course, not only for political and national reasons but because of security considerations.

Belgrade views the Croats as a security risk for another reason: In keeping with generalized Serb suspicions regarding residual loyalties to the Ustashi among Croats, the central government is very much concerned about the influence of Croat emigré publications, which have violently condemned Serb domination of the Yugoslav state in general, as well as attacking specific Yugoslav policies. Particularly worrisome to Belgrade is the influence that these groups have attempted to gain with the 300,000 Croats of draft age who are working in Western Europe.[8] Also of concern, if true, are reports that the emigrés have been working in cooperation with the Catholic church in Yugoslavia.[9] Apparently, Tito is sufficiently concerned about these groups to have sent agents to Western Europe to deal with them.[10] Even bolder was the engineering in 1975 of the kidnapping in Bucharest of Colonel Vlado Dapcevic, a high-level, allegedly pro-Soviet emigré who was subsequently interrogated and tried in Yugoslavia.[11]

It would appear that these forces abroad are quite well organized; in 1972, for example, they were able to coordinate major infiltration raids into Yugoslavia from neighboring Austria.[12] Of special significance to Belgrade must be the apparent cooperation between some of these groups and the Soviet Union. Despite Croat suspicions of alleged Serb pro-Muskovite sentiment, it has been a Croat Communist organization, the "Croatian Communist Party Abroad," which all but invited the Red Army into Yugoslavia. The politburo of this organization drafted a six-point resolution calling for a sovereign socialist Croat state, allied with the Warsaw Pact countries, and declared that the Soviet Union was obligated on the basis of "socialist solidarity to protect our national [Croatian] territory."[13] (This amounted to an invocation of the Brezhnev Doctrine.)

One consideration that could militate against overt Soviet exploitation of Yugoslavia's nationality problems—and particularly against Soviet pandering to irredentist claims upon Yugoslav territory by Tito's neighbors—is the multinational character of the USSR itself. The Soviet Union is a state (perhaps "empire" might be a more accurate description) the population of which is only about one-half Great Russian. Included among its nationalities are such actually or potentially rebellious elements as Lithuanians, Ukrainians, and Tatars. Moreover, the USSR has been subject to revisionist claims upon its territory by its own neighbors. For example, the Romanians have argued for some time—with considerable justification—that "Moldavians" actually are just Romanians called by another name, and that the Ukrainian and Moldavian SSRs include the historically Romanian regions of northern Bucovina and Bessarabia. In fact, Moldavia was the name of one of the two Danubian provinces that were combined in 1861 to form the modern Romanian state.

Perhaps of even greater consequence are the Chinese machinations with respect to Altaic nationalities within Soviet Central Asia and in the Soviet puppet state of Outer Mongolia, some of whose ethnic brethren live in the PRC. It may be questioned whether the USSR would feel at ease exposing the multiethnic Red Army to a conflict featuring a prominent display of the banner of national self-determination. Irrespective of its sensitivity (or lack thereof) to legal precedents, Moscow comprehends the perceptual significance of analogies and might be reluctant to provide political ammunition to neighbors with claims, or potential claims, to what at present is Soviet territory. Particularly would this be the case if the USSR resorted to Warsaw Pact troops in "settling the Yugoslav issue." After all, even such traditionally dependent states as Poland (the eastern portion of which was incorporated into the USSR in 1939 and again in 1944) and the "German Democratic Republic" (bearing in mind the annexation of northern East Prussia to the RSFSR) might revive territorial grievances vis-à-vis the Soviet big brother if the Warsaw Pact became involved in armed action to aid ethnic minorities in realizing their irredentist aspirations.

Nevertheless, there is evidence that the Soviet Union (albeit with rather limited success) did attempt to exploit Slovak autonomist desires before, during, and after the 1968 invasion of Czechoslovakia.[14] Thus it would appear that when the chips are down Moscow has shown willingness to resort to any available weapon, including invocation of the slogan of ethnic autonomy. However, there are qualitative differences between increased autonomy for Slovakia and, let us say, territorial dismemberment of Yugoslavia. The potentially dangerous implications for Moscow of the latter course, as analyzed here, conceivably could give the Kremlin pause, particularly in view of Soviet eagerness to "freeze" post-1945 European boundaries—a policy that achieved its desiderata at Helsinki in 1975.

What may be of more far-reaching significance than Moscow's flirtation with Croat separatism is Soviet support, since 1960, for an anti-Titoist (strongly "centralist") group in Kiev, headed by a Montenegrin named Mileta Perovitch (Perovic), who is said to be a former colonel in the Yugoslav Army. Apparently this group maintains branches in at least two other major East European cities, namely Prague and Budapest.[15]

The economic issue, which has assumed a prominent role in conflicts between the Yugoslav nationalities, is not, strictly speaking, an ethnic question but rather a matter of relations between the socialist republics. Of course, ethnic and republican boundaries in Yugoslavia do not coincide in many instances (see Appendix 1). According to the 1971 census, more than 1 million of the 4.5 million Croats in Yugoslavia do not live in Croatia, while over 600,000 Serbs do live in that republic.[16] It is not clear whether a Croat living, for example, in Serbia, may not consider his economic welfare to be tied to that of the republic of his domicile rather than to the prosperity of Croatia. Similarly, Serbs residing in Croatia may identify very strongly with Serbia on cultural and political matters while regarding their economic fortunes as being inextricably inter-twined with the welfare of Croatia.

One of the major complaints frequently lodged by representatives of Croatia and Slovenia is that they have been forced to bear singlehandedly the brunt of developing the less advanced republics (Macedonia, Bosnia-Hercegovina, and Montenegro), as well as the Kosmet. Apparently this question has led to the growth of what amounts to alliances between Serbia and the underdeveloped areas, on the one hand, and Croatia and Slovenia, on the other.[17]

A second economic issue has been the alleged favoritism shown by the central government toward large Belgrade firms. Apparently this phenomenon is related to the bitter struggle that occurred in 1966 when the archconservative secret police chief, Aleksandr Rankovic, was ousted, since such enterprises are managed to a significant extent by former members of Rankovic's secret police force.[18]

Another extremely sensitive issue in the economic realm has been the control of foreign currency balances, including the remittances of Yugoslav citizens working abroad temporarily (the so-called *Gastarbeiter*). The Croatian and Slovenian parties have stated that they should be given greater control over these balances because, as the most developed republics, they have been major producers of the export goods netting profits from abroad. The Croatian party claims that Croatia is particularly entitled to such benefits, since a disproportionately high percentage of the *Gastarbeiter* are Croats (see Appendix 2).[19]

While the economic problem was a significant irritant during the 1971 Serbo-Croat dispute, it does not appear to have been one of the immediate precipitants of the purges of Croatian Communists accused of favoring nationalism (most notably Savka Dabcevic-Kucar and Mika Tripalo) in December of that year. According to Tito, the purge was necessitated by the Croatian Communist leaders' "lack of vigilance" in allowing *Matica Hrvatska* and other Croatian cultural organizations to publicize their nationalistic and anticentralist sentiments. Their other major "crime" was allowing the universities (particularly Zagreb University) to become, allegedly, hotbeds of Croatian nationalism.[20]

Among the focal areas of conflicting aspirations which threaten to expand the scope of Serbo-Croat hostility is the situation in Bosnia-Hercegovina (the only republic lacking a predominant nationality), which finds a Croat minority of 20.6 percent outnumbered both by Moslems (39.6 percent of the total population) and by Serbs (37.2 percent).[21] The Croat portions of Bosnia-Hercegovina were joined to Croatia by the 1939 Sporazum, the short-lived Serbo-Croat compromise; however, they were separated again by Tito in 1944—a development hurtful to these Croats, who found themselves reduced once more to minority status. Equally volatile is the situation in Croatia, which contains a substantial Serb minority of 14 percent. The existence of these minorities provides fuel for local animosities that can hardly be kept secret and helps to exacerbate the conflict between the nationalities. Moreover, as demonstrated by the pro-Nazi positions taken by many German *Volksdeutsche,* minorities tend to adopt extreme nationalistic positions, a pattern which serves only to confirm the prevalent biases of the local majority.

For example, the Serb minority in Croatia comprises much of the "centralist faction" in that republic. In the wake of the events of December 1971, such a position—particularly when held by residents of Croatia—can only be anathema to most Croat inhabitants of the republic. This predominantly Serb centralist group repeatedly has been attacked by the present "moderate" leadership of Croatia (under Dr. Vladimir Bakaric) as proponents of "greater state hegemonism," the euphemism commonly used to attack Serbization programs.[22]

The existence of such minorities also renders more difficult the grant of wider autonomy to the socialist republics since the Belgrade Serbs are hardly likely, given their prejudice against Croats, to leave their Serbian brethren in Croatia to the mercy of forces allegedly descended from the Ustashi. For that matter, Croat minorities in Bosnia-Hercegovina and Serbia may be inclined no less to lobby strenuously against a policy of complete decentralization in favor of the socialist republics in which they happen to be outnumbered.

Thus, long-standing biases, exacerbated by local antipathies, combine with national, economic, and political issues practically to guarantee continuation of the feud between Serbs and Croats. Tito's 1971 purges ousted the more outspoken nationalists from the leadership of the Croatian party and, to a lesser degree, the party of other republics. However, by no means did he eliminate nationalism among the Croat and Serb masses. Should Tito's demise weaken the central leadership in any way, Croats well may seek to ameliorate what they consider to be their plight by resorting to violence—directed in part, perhaps, against the local Serb minority. Such a reaction might lead to a confrontation with the Yugoslav army, to reprisals against the Croat minorities living outside the republic of Croatia, and possibly to attempts by other groups, both national and ideological in orientation, to exploit the turmoil and overthrow the status quo. Even if foreign powers did not interfere, the resulting anarchy well might destroy the Yugoslav state as now constituted.

Although Slovenes have been aggrieved too, they are far less likely to initiate violence—simply because Slovenia is a relatively homogenous republic and most Slovenes live in Slovenia.[23] While Slovene resentment of the central government rarely has taken on the intensity of Croat sentiments vis-à-vis Belgrade, nevertheless there have been periodic murmurings of discontent by the highly advanced and somewhat "Central-

Europeanized" Slovene population—most notably during 1976, when two prominent Slovenes were jailed essentially for expressions of Slovene nationalism. One of the individuals concerned, Victor Blazic, a journalist for the Slovenian Communist Party paper *Delo* (although not a member of the Communist Party himself), was sentenced on September 16, 1976, to two years imprisonment for having written an article for *Zaliv,* a Slovene-language magazine published in Trieste, which urged greater political freedom in Slovenia.[24] The prosecution and subsequent sentencing (to six years' imprisonment) of a second Slovene, Franc Miklavcic, may be of far greater significance; Miklavcic, a judge in Slovenia, was sentenced for harboring alleged separatist sentiments— evidence of which was derived mainly from inferential passages in his personal diary confiscated by the police.[25] The Miklavcic case may be indicative of more than increased tensions between the federal government and the Slovenes; it is interesting that Miklavcic's conviction came only a few months after a Belgrade defense attorney, Srdja Popovic, was sentenced to a year in prison essentially for defending a dissident client too vigorously. Although Popovic's sentence later was suspended, he was barred from practicing law for one year.[26] Moreover, there was considerable evidence that Jovan Barovic, a defense counselor for the noted Yugoslav writer and dissident Mihajlo Mihajlov, was harassed during Mihajlov's trial in 1975.[27] Thus, one element of the increased repression in Yugoslavia may be the systematic elimination of any flicker of independence revealed by Yugoslavs connected with the judiciary. However, this raises the whole issue of renewed repression in Yugoslavia, which is discussed in the next chapter.

3
The Struggle with the New Left

When the Yugoslav government began to centralize (and, some would say, to Stalinize) the Yugoslav system after the December 1971 purges, there was a strong reaction from liberal, idealistic Marxists, who criticized the movement away from more progressive forms of "self-management."[1] This "New Left" opposition gathered around the Zagreb philosophical bimonthly *Praxis* and the Belgrade journal *Philosofija*.[2] The movement generally is called the *Praxis* group, in reference to the first and most influential of the liberal journals.

This group, although under constant attack by the central government, considers itself to be fervently Titoist. Its members frequently refer to themselves as "the best Titoists," in the tradition of the November 1952 Sixth Party Congress. (At that meeting Tito rejected Stalinism in the most resolute and unambiguous fashion.) The "New Left" has voiced support continuously for Tito's original concept of "creative and self-management socialism."[3] Nonetheless, following three years of reprimands and thinly veiled threats by the Serbian and Yugoslav leaderships, eight "New Left" professors were ousted from Belgrade University in January of 1975 for "anti-self-management" activities.[4]

How is it possible that such faithful Titoists could be ousted by Tito? It appears that this is really a case of Tito departing from Titoism. The calls by *Praxis* for democratization and decentralization of the party—leading finally to a "withering away of the party" once envisaged by Lenin himself—are not at all inconsistent with the spirit of the Sixth Party Congress. It is Tito who has recentralized the party and, according to the "New Left," it is he who has become a "charismatic leader" in the tradition of the Stalinist "cult of the personality."[5] It is ironic that the most loyal adherents to the 1958 Yugoslav Party Program (because of which Tito was condemned by Moscow for revisionism) and the most consistent opponents of "Stalinist bureaucracy" are accused now by Tito himself of right wing deviationism.[6] It appears that the basis of Tito's rejection of this group is his fear of losing personal power, were there to take place a true de-Stalinization in Yugoslavia, complete with debureaucratization, decentralization, greater freedom of expression, and elimination of any cult of the personality.

There have been attempts to link the Zagreb journal to the Croatian nationalists by means of the accusation that *Praxis* was promoting a "mass movement," the same argument which at times was used against the subsequently purged Croatian leadership.[7] However, the "New Left" does not appear to have a mass base, nor has it embraced nationalistic doctrines. Most of its supporters appear to be intellectuals, with sizable numbers of Serb and Slovene professors and students joining their Croat peers. Indeed, *Praxis* consistently opposed the purged Croat nationalist leaders, precisely because of their nationalism,[8] as well as clashing with the present Croat leadership on ideological issues.[9] Actually, the *Praxis* group has emphasized that Croat nationalism is no less an antithesis of the Marxist precept of the "withering away of the state" than is

Yugoslav centralism.[10]

Perhaps it is a pity that the "New Left" in Yugoslavia is not the mass movement that Tito has accused it of being. Although the group must have some strength, else probably it would not have lasted so long, it is hardly conceivable that a liberal, almost utopian group of professors ever could muster a degree of power comparable to that of the various nationalist movements. To date, the greatest show of force ever mustered by the "New Left" was the 1973 threat by Belgrade University students to strike if the eight professors were fired.[11] Thus, despite the wealth of publicity that it has received, both in the West and in Yugoslavia, it seems improbable that the "New Left" could have a major impact on the outcome of any foreseeable post-Tito domestic power struggle. Of course, if there were to be an invasion of Yugoslavia, then, judging by the Hungarian and Czechoslovak experiences, it is precisely the idealists of the "New Left" type who might constitute the catalyst for resistance.

4
Government in the Post-Tito Era

In keeping with the trend in recent years toward centralization of the Yugoslav political system, Yugoslavia's 140-member Chamber of Nationalities, the de facto senior body within Yugoslavia's old five-house assembly system, in 1974 proclaimed the country's fourth constitution. Although designed ostensibly to strengthen workers' self-management, actually the document will serve to reinforce countrywide control by the LCY (the Communist Party) and to increase the political influence of the Yugoslav army.[1]

According to the new system, all adult Yugoslav citizens may vote in three different capacities (see Appendix 3). First, as consumers, they may vote for delegates to Chambers of Local Communities (that form part of Communal Assemblies, at the lowest local level) and to Chambers of Communes (that form part of the higher-level Assemblies of the two autonomous provinces and the six socialist republics). Second, in their role as members of their professions, they may elect delegates to Communal, Provincial, and Republican Chambers of Associated Labor. Finally, as members of socio-political organizations (primarily the LCY), they may elect delegates to Communal, Republican, and Provincial Socio-Political Chambers. From among these three groups of delegates the actual membership is chosen of the various chambers mentioned.[2]

The Communal Assemblies are responsible for conducting relevant activities at the local level and also for electing the 220-member Federal Chamber of the (two-chamber) Assembly of the SFRY, the all-Yugoslav chamber responsible for legislation which does not require approval by the autonomous provinces and socialist republics. The Provincial and Republican Assemblies are responsible for electing the 88-member Chamber of Republics and Autonomous Provinces, the second house of the Assembly of the SFRY, which is responsible for legislation that does require Republican and Provincial approval.[3]

While it might appear that the average citizen thus would be given a significant role in the political process, in reality this is not the case. The major innovation limiting the power of the citizenry and of the delegates within this pyramidal structure is the "imperative mandate," which inhibits delegates to the assemblies from voting their consciences, but rather compels them to vote in accordance with the desires of "the base" they represent. The delegates are "advised" as to what these wishes are by the LCY—which, thus, in reality remains the repository of power. Similarly, the party, in fact, is responsible for the supervision of the elections and for the voting performance of members in the two chambers of the Assembly of the SFRY. Thus, regardless of which persons are elected, their "decisions" are preordained.[4] In effect, therefore, the party directly controls the socio-political chambers and, indirectly, the other chambers, as well as the selection process for the two houses of the all-Yugoslav Assembly of the SFRY.

In addition, delegates to the lower assemblies are not to be privy to information on all matters. Moreover, it has been emphasized that there is to be regular, rapid, and massive turnover in membership of the local assemblies. Thus, in effect, Yugoslavia has professionalized governance at the top, power-less, amateur, pro forma representation at the base, and a powerful, centralized, party apparatus supervising and running the system as a whole.[5]

In addition to the two chambers of the Assembly of the SFRY at the federal level, the constitution provides for a State Presidency. This is a body of nine persons: six from each republic, plus one each from the Vojvodina and the Kosmet, in addition to the president of the LCY, who serves as an ex officio member.[6] Under this formula, it might be feasible for Serbs to control as many as five out of the nine votes: one each for Serbia, Montenegro, Vojvodina (where Serbs now are in a majority), Bosnia (where Serbs almost equal Moslems in number), and for the leader of the LCY, should he be a Serb. The office of president of the SFRY is rotated among representatives of the eight socialist republics and provinces who serve in the State Presidency. Each president serves for two years and each area must be represented in turn.[7] Thus, it would seem that the president of Yugoslavia, in his individual capacity, would not necessarily enjoy great personal power, particularly compared with the leader of the LCY—who, presumably, can serve an unlimited term in office.

However, the State Presidency as a body is endowed with considerable power. It is able to present proposals to the Assembly of the SFRY; if these recommendations are not accepted within nine months, the Presidency may dissolve the two chambers and rule by itself, until a new Assembly is chosen, at which point the Presidency is to be dissolved.[8] It seems likely that the Presidency, which consists of persons of considerable stature, would find it far easier as a group to ensure its reelection in the event of such conflict than could the members of an uncooperative Assembly of the SFRY.

Another group that has been strengthened considerably is the Yugoslav army, which has been granted an expanded role in the LCY. For example, in 1974, 12 percent of the members of the LCY Central Committee came from the army (as compared to about 6 percent in 1964). Moreover, for the first time, army representatives in that committee will be chosen by the LCY Army Organization and not by the rest of the Central Committee.[9] Clearly, the army is seen as a key to Yugoslavia's future and, as such, is being given a greater stake in maintaining the present system. Moreover, close and interlocking relationships continue to be fostered between the army and the party. In the armed forces, 36 percent are party members, including "more than 90 percent" of the NCOs and 98.5 percent of the officers. In the all-powerful Secretariat of the LCY Army Organization, ethnic Serbs and their Montenegrin kin predominate, with a total of six of the eleven Secretariat members. Here, as in other Yugoslav key posts, the Montenegrins—the "purest of the Serbs"—enjoy their usual disproportionate influence dating back to the period of the Partisans (with two out of the eleven Secretariat members, Montenegrins constitute 18.2 percent, while comprising a mere 2.5 percent of the total Yugoslav population).[10]

A new streamlined Politburo and Secretariat of the LCY reportedly are to be chosen at the party's Eleventh Congress in 1978, with a special place on the planned seven-member Politburo being reserved for the army (probably to be filled by a Serb, the minister of defense, General Nikola Ljubicic). Presumably key party and state positions will be concentrated in the hands of a few core leaders. Serb, and, particularly, Montenegrin predominance is marked both in the leadership of the party (e.g., 6 Montenegrins in the 48-member LCY

Presidium) and in its membership.[11] Thus, the ethnically Serb areas, Serbia proper, the Vojvodina (where Serbs now constitute the majority), and Montenegro, with altogether 37.67 percent of the total population of Yugoslavia, comprise 46.33 percent of LCY membership. Comparing the ratios for various regions (of their respective percentages of total party membership to their percentages of total population) reveals an astoundingly high indicator of 155 for Montenegro, 127 for the Vojvodina, and 118 for Serbia proper, as compared to a mere 90 for Croatia, 86 for Bosnia and Macedonia, 81 for Slovenia, and less than 79 for Kosovo.[12]

A similar picture emerges from the composition of the central government: of the 15-member core of the executive (the premier, four deputy premiers, and ten ministers without portfolio) 8 are Serbs and Montenegrins, with the latter holding no less than 3 positions, including the premiership itself (Veselin Djuranovic).[13]

The role of the party leader naturally will be central during the post-Tito era. It is most important that Tito's successor in this capacity should meet several criteria. First, preferably he should not be a Serb himself, since other nationalities might view his accession as indicative of a new attempt at ensuring Serb hegemony over the party and the state. At the same time, he must be acceptable to the Serbs, as the largest and most powerful nationality. Finally, he must enjoy the support and respect of the army in view of its increasingly vital role, particularly during the succession period.[14] However, even a personality meeting all of these qualifications may have great difficulty maintaining the Yugoslav state in its present form.

Part 2

International Implications

5
The Soviet Attitude toward Yugoslavia

The key to Yugoslavia's future is likely to be the behavior of the Soviet Union during the period following Tito's exit from the scene. Yugoslavia and the Soviet Union achieved a degree of rapprochement during the 1960s that suffered traumatic interruption in 1968 as a result of the Soviet invasion of Czechoslovakia, the promulgation of the Brezhnev Doctrine, and the subsequent joint Yugoslav-Romanian stand against Moscow. The rapprochement was resumed in the early 1970s and appeared even to be flourishing by 1973, although Belgrade continued to be haunted by the specter of 1968. An indication of the degree of cooperation reached in 1973 is the agreement between the two countries which provided for the Soviet shipment to Yugoslavia of moderate quantities of Mi-8 helicopters, Yak-40 airplanes, aviation fuel, roller bearings, and other goods of potential military value.[1] However, since that time relations have deteriorated as a consequence of interrelated diplomatic and domestic considerations in both capitals.

On the diplomatic front, the Yugoslavs have infuriated Moscow by standing at the forefront of a coalition of Southern European Communist parties, including the Romanians and, to a lesser degree, the Italian and Spanish parties.[2] This group has opposed attempts by the Soviet Union to use the proposed European Communist Conference to reestablish the CPSU as the "world Communist center," thereby undermining the Yugoslav "separate road to socialism."[3] When the long-awaited meeting of Communist parties finally materialized in the summer of 1976, President Tito issued statements asserting "the principles of independence, equality and noninterference as the basis of cooperation among Communist and workers' parties," voicing opposition to "all forms of interference in the internal affairs of other countries" and criticising the concept of "spheres of influence."[4] This position—which took dead aim at the basic diplomatic goals and policies of the Soviet Union—could not be very pleasing to the USSR, to put it mildly. Moreover, the Yugoslavs have been unwilling to accept the USSR's attempts to utilize that meeting and similar conferences as a forum to condemn the Chinese for what Moscow views as their major transgressions. This Yugoslav attitude, shared by the Romanian party, found expression in the Romanian leadership's statement that the participants in the 1976 conference "should not criticize or blame any other Communist parties, regardless of whether they are or are not attending the conference."[5] Furthermore, the CPSU cannot have been overjoyed at the Bijedic trip to China, and his affirmation of Yugoslav support for the Chinese policy of "antihegemonism."

Domestically, the Yugoslav government has been experiencing problems with "Cominformists," who have opposed Tito's autonomist foreign policy—suggesting, in its stead, Yugoslav subservience to the USSR or at least more intimate policy coordination.[6] The situation was exacerbated in the mid-1970s by a sharp increase in the magnitude and scope of confrontation between the Yugoslav secret police (UDBA) and "Cominformists" (or "Neo-cominformists") both within Yugoslavia and abroad. Most notable was the 1975 kidnapping in Bucharest of Colonel Vlado Dapcevic, a Yugoslav emigré, who was alleged by Belgrade authorities to have been working in collusion with Soviet security organs in an attempt to undermine the Yugoslav state as it is currently constituted.[7]

That the "Cominformists" apparently contain significant Serb and Montenegrin elements is not surprising in view of the fact that, traditionally, communism in Yugoslavia (which, until Tito's expulsion from the Cominform in June of 1948, belonged to the extreme militant, "leftist" variety both in domestic and international policies) has been dominated ethnically by Serbs and Montenegrins. This factor compounds the list of dangers confronting post-Tito Yugoslavia; i.e., a Serb-Montenegrin Muscovite faction might request Soviet aid to move against other groups in Belgrade or against separatist movements in non-Serb republics and provinces. The marked numerical predominance of Serb and Montenegrin officers in the Yugoslav armed forces and security services (a heritage from the Rankovic period) contributes substantially to the dimensions of these dangers.

It seems that significant centers of "Cominformist" activity have been established in Budapest, Prague, and Kiev. From these bases, a former Yugoslav colonel named Mileta Perovitch (Perovic), along with a Professor Bogdan Javovic, appear to be directing an East European anti-Titoist network as well as heading a "Communist Party of Yugoslavia" in Moscow, with branches in Yugoslavia (serving presumably as a foil to Tito's party, the League of Communists of Yugoslavia). In Western Europe, there has been considerable Cominformist activity in Belgium (where Colonel Dapcevic had gained citizenship prior to being kidnapped), the Federal Republic of Germany, and Switzerland. The Yugoslav secret police have been operating against Cominformists and other emigrés both in Eastern and Western Europe—apparently engendering considerable ill will toward Yugoslavia because of these activities. In fact, the security organs of the German Federal Republic have been compelled to establish a special branch of the Wiesbaden office in charge of non-German criminal offenders so as to keep an eye on the triangular "operations," gangland style, of Cominformists (KGB), UDBA, and Ustashi, particularly among Yugoslav (predominantly Croat) migrant workers (*Gastarbeiter*).[8] (With barely 1 percent of the population of the FRG, Yugoslavs constituted more than one in thirty-seven of all murder suspects in that country in 1975 and more than one in twenty-one of all suspects in cases of violence, including poisoning, leading to grave injury.)[9]

The "Communist Party of Yugoslavia" actually managed, in 1974, to hold a secret, relatively large-scale congress at Bar, Montenegro, an event which precipitated a series of massive arrests when discovered by Tito. Early in 1976, this group released an extensive action program including the following provisions:

- formation of a united National Front of all socialist and democratic parties and groups opposed to Tito;
- formation of a provisional government of all parties;
- disbandment of the secret police and the counterintelligence organizations in the army and militia and the abolition of all concentration camps and political prisons;
- abolition of the presidency of the republic, dismissal of Marshal Tito from all ruling functions, prohibition of his political activity, and confiscation of the property he has obtained illegally;
- nationalization of the principal means of production;
- a new electoral law giving every adult the right to vote, irrespective of his political views, and elections for a consti-

tutional assembly within twelve months;
• Yugoslavia to leave the Balkan Pact—"a part of the aggressive Atlantic Pact"—and to withdraw from agreements made with Western governments.[10]

These provisions certainly would not appear calculated to endear Moscow to Tito.[11]

Particularly annoying to the Yugoslav government must be the apparently close contacts between the Soviet Union and both nationalist forces within Yugoslavia and nationalist emigrés. A development of great concern to Belgrade undoubtedly was the resolution drawn up by the Politburo of the "Croatian Communist Party Abroad," which suggested the prospect of Soviet military intervention in Croatia. The resolution stated that the Soviet Union was obligated on the basis of "socialist solidarity to protect our national [Croatian] territory." (This meant, in fact, application of the language of the Brezhnev Doctrine to Yugoslav soil.) The resolution went on to say that "every attack on our territory is at the same time an attack on the Soviet Red Army."[12] Belgrade has accused the Soviet Union of stirring up unrest among nationalist groups within Yugoslavia, and suspects that Moscow may be preparing the ground for being "invited in" to aid a separatist group.[13] Similarly, the Yugoslav government hardly can be delighted at Russian support for Bulgaria's line on the Macedonian question.[14]

The Soviet leaders, on their part, must be irritated by the Yugoslav policy of publishing works by Solzhenitsyn banned in the USSR, particularly since the men in Belgrade are the only ruling Communist leaders to do so.[15] In general, the Yugoslavs probably have infuriated Moscow almost as much with their relative liberalism in publishing what the Soviet government considers to be "heretical" materials as by their state and party foreign policy transgressions.

Admittedly, Yugoslav-Soviet relations currently are by no

means at their lowest ebb. In spring 1975 the late prime minister Bijedic visited the Soviet Union in response to a visit Kosygin made to Belgrade in September 1973. This trip dealt mostly with economic matters and resulted in the extension of further Soviet credits to Yugoslavia.[16] Moreover, there have been reports that the Soviet navy has been granted docking privileges in Yugoslavia, a development which seems to contradict the apparent deepening of the Soviet-Yugoslav rift indicated by the Cominformist trials of the mid-1970s.[17]

Perhaps Tito feels that a policy of simultaneous appeasement and deterrence of the Soviet Union is suitable under existing circumstances. Nevertheless, the Soviet Union is likely to be tempted at an opportune moment to liquidate the three-decade-old sore spot in Eastern Europe, in which case post-Tito Yugoslavia will be in serious danger. On two prior occasions, the Russians have chosen to engage in direct military intervention in Communist countries; neither Czechoslovakia nor even Hungary had been half as troublesome or defiant as Yugoslavia repeatedly has proven to be. Yugoslavia's defense capabilities in such a contingency are discussed in a subsequent chapter of this book. However, it is necessary first to consider the implications of possible Soviet intervention for the states on NATO's southern flank and for the NATO-Warsaw Pact balance as a whole.

6

Regional Implications of Soviet Intervention

It is conjectural what would be the implications for NATO's southern flank of Soviet ventures resulting in a significant increase of Moscow's power in and around Yugoslavia. Equally speculative would be an assessment of the reaction of NATO's southern members to less overt, although equally successful, Soviet efforts on behalf of Yugoslav factions favorable to the Russian position.

Italy

In the case of Italy, it would be advisable not to discount the possibility of an instinctive recoil by the Italian electorate from the spectacle of Soviet domination of Yugoslavia, particularly the Adriatic coast and the Slovenian hinterland of Trieste.[1] Such a reaction might reverse, to some degree, the trend of recent years toward increased support by the Italian voting public for parties of the far left. This development would render less likely the realization of the "historic compromise" wherein the parties of the center would be forced, by virtue of the number of seats held by the PCI (Italian Communist Party) in the Italian Parliament, to accept a coalition government including significant Communist participation on the Cabinet level. It is possible, however, to overstate the sensitivity of the Italian electorate to Soviet moves and perhaps to foreign affairs in general. Following the brutal Soviet invasion of Czechoslovakia in 1968 (an act that was condemned by the PCI and by many other Western Communist parties, including the French, as well as by the Yugoslav, Romanian, and even the normally loyal Finnish CP), far leftist Italian political parties did register some setbacks at the polls.[2] However, the losses incurred were by no means of a cataclysmic nature. The diminution of electoral strength suffered by the PCI and its closest ally, the leftist splinter PSIUP, was only marginal; their joint strength slipped from 31.4 percent of the total vote to 29.2 percent between the May 1968 national elections, held immediately prior to the invasion, and the May 1970 regional elections. Moreover, most of that loss was suffered not by the PCI (whose vote fell by less than 1 percent, from 26.9 percent in 1968 to 26.0 percent in 1970), but rather by the PSIUP, which declined precipitously for a small party (from 4.5 percent to 3.2 percent, a loss of no less than 29 percent of its previous share of the vote).[3] Since a "protest" vote against Soviet policy probably would have been registered directly at the expense of the PCI, and not of its ally, it is likely that at least some proportion of the decline in popularity of the far left in Italy during that period may be attributed to domestic issues or other situational variables. Of course, since Yugoslavia borders on Italy, a significant change in the Yugoslav status quo might be viewed by Italians with less equanimity than was the invasion of Czechoslovakia.

Needless to say, the implications of Soviet actions in Yugoslavia for PCI electoral strength would reflect, at least to some degree, the party's pronouncements at the time. Strong PCI condemnation of Soviet interference in Yugoslavia might mitigate to some degree the reaction of the Italian voting population against parties of the far left. It might be questioned, however, whether, on an issue of such importance, the traditionalists (or, perhaps more precisely, Stalinists) in the party would be prepared to allow the PCI to adopt a line of unqualified condemnation of the Soviet Union and the Warsaw Pact. Perhaps the "hard-liners" in the party, who have remained remarkably subdued during recent years of apparent PCI moderation (a phenomenon that some suspect constitutes merely a tactic by which the party seeks to dissemble its way to power), would emerge into the open and insist upon a less anti-Soviet position. Such a development might lead to a rupture within the party, between "Euro-Communists" and "hard-liners." On the other hand, if the seemingly "moderate" policy line of the PCI really has been a smoke screen all along, the more old-fashioned elements, recognizing an opportunity to lend still further credibility to the PCI's "autonomous" position, might opt for a "soft" public stance in order not to vitiate the effect of years of subterfuge.

Were the Soviet Union sufficiently sophisticated to engage in a certain amount of "creative" diplomacy, it might actually manage matters in such a way that Soviet adventurism in Yugoslavia might redound to the benefit of the PCI. If the USSR were interested in helping the PCI, and if the Russian aim were to dismember Yugoslavia, rather than to keep it intact under the aegis of a pro-Moscow regime, the Kremlin—taking great care to advertise the crucial role of the PCI as an intermediary—might arrange to settle the long-standing Yugoslav-Italian border disagreements to the advantage of the Italian state.[4] Thus, the PCI might emerge, in the wake of a

Soviet thrust into Yugoslavia, as an effective Italian nationalistic party.

While this particular scenario might appear far-fetched, it does illustrate that it may be possible for the USSR to take actions in Yugoslavia, even of an extreme nature, without necessarily crippling the PCI. As against this consideration, the argument most damaging to the PCI cause, in the wake of any Russian adventurism in Yugoslavia, would be that no Communist state, regardless of its attempts to avoid provoking Moscow (as Tito has tried on many occasions in recent years) could be considered safe from Soviet interference. Nor would "neutrality" or "nonalignment" constitute a safeguard, since a PCI-controlled Italy could hardly go much further to place itself outside the confines of the Soviet bloc than Tito went during the years after his expulsion from the Cominform (e.g., by joining the Balkan Pact). Nevertheless, the argument would continue, Yugoslavia had found itself a victim of Soviet interference. The only counterargument would be to point to the formal distinction between a "nonaligned" Yugoslavia and an Italian state which, even under PCI leadership, did not abrogate its membership in NATO.

Of course, it might be questioned whether the Soviet Union really might be pained to witness a decline in the PCI's electoral strength. The Italian Communists have long deviated from the Soviet line on issues of some importance to the Russian leadership. As early as 1956 the PCI, under the leadership of Palmiro Togliatti, espoused "polycentrism" within the international communist movement, although significantly it did not venture to oppose the Soviet invasion of Hungary that year. During an earlier period, the Italian Communist leader Antonio Gramsci had disdained the use of the traditional Marxist term "dictatorship of the proletariat," preferring the use of the milder phrase "hegemony of the working class."[5] More recent PCI pronouncements have been moderately nonconformist from the Soviet standpoint. However, some observers question the sincerity of the apparent increase in PCI deviation from Moscow's positions. Despite seeming defiance of attempts by the Kremlin to reassert its position as the "first among equals" at the 1976 East Berlin conference of European Communist parties, sufficient caveats and qualifications have been attached to PCI policy statements to warrant considerable suspicion regarding the party's genuine commitment to "moderation."[6] For example, the much-publicized PCI statement condoning an Italian role in NATO did not present as great a departure from the expected orthodox behavior pattern of an obedient Moscovite party as might be presumed. While certainly it is true that the PCI has switched from its former unqualified "NATO out!" position, the party's new stance permits merely that Italy should remain in a "changed" NATO.[7] For example, the party's newspaper *L'Unità* wrote in 1976 that "the Communists of Italy or any other country could not accept the Atlantic Pact as it is, especially insofar as it is one of the instruments of American tampering with the policy of our country and of Western Europe."[8] The implication seems to be that the Italian Communists are demanding changes which would include a serious reduction of the American presence in NATO. Coming, as it would, during a period when the British and others are retrenching militarily, such a policy could only undermine further the efficacy of a NATO which some observers already are questioning. One indication that the Soviet Union might be viewing the PCI somewhat more positively than many Western observers assume was a recent Brezhnev statement in *Pravda* condemning the United States and other Western countries for throttling Italy by reportedly refusing to grant loans to any Italian government which included Communist participation.[9] While this statement may have been intended merely to gain a debating point at the expense of the West, its effect was also to

portray the PCI as a nationalistic Italian party being undermined by foreign interference.

Whatever the actual implications of Soviet activities in
Yugoslavia for the future of the PCI, it should be recalled that
on many occasions in the past the Soviet Union has proved
willing to sacrifice the interests of nonruling foreign Communist parties, at least in the short run, for the sake of furthering
Soviet state interests. Several examples of this policy preference come to mind. Specifically, the Soviet Union abandoned
the Turkish Communist Party to oppression and even execu-
tions by Kemalist forces during 1921-23, when the USSR was
flirting with Kemal Atatürk; similarly, the Soviet-dominated
Comintern ordered the Chinese Communists to ally themselves with their Kuomintang adversaries during 1921-27 and
again during the period 1937-45, after the Sian Incident. More
recently, the Soviet Union cooperated in the "voluntary dissolution" of the Egyptian Communist Party during the decade
1965-75.

Perhaps the Soviet Union even might welcome a reaction
against the PCI, which could serve to purge the party of
elements favoring an unqualified "Euro-Communist" position.
From the Soviet standpoint, a party consisting of loyal Mosco-
vites and other "traditionalists" might be far more manageable
and hence more useful from the Soviet perspective than a
larger but more heterogeneous and unruly communist party.
In that sense, any Soviet action on the international front
which served to purge the PCI of marginal elements, rather
than being viewed as a negative development by the Kremlin,
actually might be regarded as a galvanizing action, prodding
the Italian party back into Leninist parameters.

While Soviet activity vis-à-vis Yugoslavia might be constrained by fear of an adverse reaction in Italy to Russian
adventurism so close to Italian soil, it is by no means certain
that concern about the probable impact on Italy would be a

prime consideration in reaching the ultimate Soviet decision. However, it may be assumed that the implications of such a move for the PCI and for other Western European Communist parties and organizations well might play a significant role in affecting the positions taken by certain individual members of the CPSU Politburo and Secretariat. Probably it would be in the interests of Soviet leaders in charge of relations with foreign, particularly non-ruling, European Communist parties and West European Communist trade unions (at present M. A. Suslov and B. N. Ponamarev) to espouse a moderate line, since they would be directly concerned in ensuring that the size and influence of their "constituents" did not decline. In this connection, a brief discussion of the decision-making pattern of the Soviet leadership is required.

The widely held assumption that Politburo voting necessarily follows consistent ideological patterns has not been supported by information available to Western analysts. Rather, many Sovietologists feel that factional struggles in the collective leadership operate on the basis of two other factors. First, the factions seem to coalesce and part ways kaleidoscopically, operating on the basis of a personal struggle for power and influence, rather than on any particular consistent ideological lines or specific issue orientations. It appears that members of the Politburo focus their factional struggles on tactically advantageous issues, rather than the issues determining the factions. Thus, each coalition of Politburo members reflects the interests of the individuals concerned in preventing their personal adversaries from successfully promoting issues with which these rivals have become strongly identified. The adoption of a policy specifically linked to one man (or one group) generally is perceived within the Soviet Union as reflecting an increase in his (or its) influence and power vis-à-vis various opponents. Since real power reflects such perceptions, it is crucial to the political career of a Soviet leader to ensure that no policies be adopted which might be regarded as issues backed by his opponents, lest this development be deemed to mark a shift in the internal Soviet balance of power. Thus, merely by virtue of their adversaries' support for a position, other Politburo members may oppose it.[10]

The second element in the Soviet decision-making process is the question of departmental interests. According to several sources, leading Soviet cadres, at least to some extent, tend to be turned into captives or mouthpieces of the institutions with which they are associated. Since each leader's subordinates also constitute his power base, he must reflect their views to some extent if he is going to maintain his own power. As one author puts it, "The Soviet political structure has a strongly 'feudal' pattern, with each top personality investing subordinates whenever possible with power and positions in return for personal 'fealty' and allegiance."[11] Thus, a second component in the personal influence of individual Soviet political figures is their ability to promote the interests of their loyal subordinates, thereby increasing their own power.

In sum, seemingly "ideological" positions adopted on important issues generally will be a reflection not of personal ideological predilections, but of various Soviet leaders' political obligations to their subordinates and allies, and, perhaps more importantly, their interests in maintaining the delicate balance of power which has existed in the Politburo since the ouster of Khrushchev—although, of late, Brezhnev has succeeded in elevating himself above that plateau. Thus, factional struggles, even if orchestrated through "ideological" debate, in many cases actually are resolved on the basis of personal expediency.[12]

To adapt this general paradigm of decision-making to the military-political realm, one needs merely to assume that the adoption of any decision dynamic enough to constitute a qualitative change in Soviet policy would enhance the political position of those most identified with that policy, should it prove successful. Moreover, whenever such policies have been adopted (e.g., during the Cuban Missile Crisis of 1962, during the invasion of Czechoslovakia in 1968, and possibly when the USSR in 1970 dispatched pilots to the Middle East), those opposed reportedly have gone on record as stating that possible gains to be made might not justify the risks involved. Thus, should such ventures prove unsuccessful, the group which was "dovish" in this context would have a perfect opportunity to brand the "hawks" as adventurists—a most powerful pejorative in the Marxist-Leninist vocabulary.[13] "Dovishness" in such situations, therefore, generally expressed in careful caveats rather than dogmatic fulminations, may be motivated largely by the desire to "clip the wings" of the *primus inter pares*.[14]

The most likely focus for internal debates is this question of risk. Thus, the "moderate" factions probably will attempt to demonstrate that American passive acquiescence in a proposed Soviet "forward" move is not guaranteed. In that manner, they would place the onus of proving the safety of the suggested venture upon their adversaries. In such a situation any credible American threat of reprisal, if accompanied by orchestration of American willingness to take action, could significantly aid the "soft-line" cause. Thus, even if the Soviet leaders believed that there was but a 5 percent chance of America taking action, considering the enormous costs inherent in a Soviet-American nuclear confrontation, such a possibility of an American military response might prove prohibitively high to the "hard-liners"—whose position in the government would be severely impaired were they to be proven wrong by subsequent events.[15] On the other hand, should the U.S. fail to provide any evidence of determination to prevent Soviet gains, then the "hawks" in Moscow could turn around and accuse the "doves" of capitulation (i.e., failure to exploit available advantages

over the West, which could have accelerated the fall of capital-
ism).

A case can be made that precisely such debates occurred in
the Kremlin during 1968, when, in demonstrative fashion, the
Soviet Union conducted Warsaw Pact maneuvers along the
borders first of Czechoslovakia and then of Romania. There
was no apparent American response to the implicit threats to
Czechoslovakia before the Soviet divisions actually moved in.
However, when President Johnson reacted to the Romanian
crisis with his famous "don't unleash the dogs of war" statement, no Soviet invasion of Romania was forthcoming. Although these episodes do not necessarily reflect the modalities
of Soviet factional debate, they do illustrate the Soviet tenden-
cy toward caution when faced with a clear danger of a U.S.
military response.

In the case of the Soviet thrust into Czechoslovakia, we do
have indications that there was indeed a factional struggle in
the Kremlin. Several sources have reported that the "hard-line"
faction in this case was led by Brezhnev himself. He was
apparently opposed in the Politburo by M. A. Suslov, A. N.
Shelepin, and A. N. Kosygin, among others.[16] Suslov had
vested interests in opposing the "forward" policy, as the man in
charge of Soviet policy toward foreign, including nonruling,
Communist parties.[17] Since the Soviet invasion could be
expected to engender bitterness against the USSR throughout
Europe, in all likelihood this development would mean some
loss of strength for Western Communist parties. Thus, in his
capacity as a "feudal" chieftain, Suslov naturally would have
wanted to avoid policies which could injure his "clients."

Kosygin, on the other hand, had no such institutional
reasons for opposing Brezhnev. In his case, his subsequent
decline vis-à-vis Brezhnev indicates that some personal factors
may have come into play. During the late 1960s, the fact that
Brezhnev was proven correct in his assessment of the lack of

risk involved in invading Czechoslovakia well may have been a major factor in his ability to surpass Kosygin.

Shelepin, too, was involved in a major power struggle with Brezhnev. As the former KGB chief, Shelepin had a tremendous potential power base including the secret police and the Komsomol, which he had also headed, However, Brezhnev was able to deprive him of power—first by replacing Shelepin's ally Semichastny with Yu. V. Andropov, a protégé of the party secretary, as KGB chief, and then by demoting Shelepin altogether.[18]

Significantly, the Kosygin-Shelepin-Suslov group could not be considered a coherent faction. Although all three generally were classified as "Stalinists," Kosygin and Suslov are two long-term adversaries, having come from diametrically opposed backgrounds: Kosygin hailed from the Zhdanov-Voznesensky group, while Suslov was one of the leaders of the anti-Voznesensky opposition.[19] It is interesting also that the three supposedly "hard-line Stalinists"—including Shelepin, former chief of the KGB—constituted the "doves" in this case, whereas the allegedly more "moderate" Khrushchevite, Brezhnev, led the "hard-liners."

Thus, during a putative internal Kremlin debate concerning the merits of a potential Soviet thrust into Yugoslavia, the question of the implications of such an action for the PCI and for Italian Communist trade unions most likely would gain significance only to the extent that Politburo members with interests in these Italian organizations (as well as their temporary factional allies) might tend to espouse a relatively cautious line. However, for the rest of the Soviet leadership, the issue probably would be far less clear-cut. As has been pointed out earlier, it is questionable whether the other Soviet leaders would view the future of the PCI as more important than major gains to be made on the geostrategic front by seizing control of Yugoslav bases. Second, some elements in the Russian regime, in view of the "revisionist" nature of the public line promulgated by the Italian Communists, might not consider it a negative development if marginal elements in the PCI dropped out, leaving a more traditionalist hard core to direct the party. Third, the Soviet leadership might not be convinced that such a Yugoslav venture would lead inevitably to long-term setbacks for the PCI. Regardless of the immediate implications for the PCI, the Soviet Union also might feel that, ultimately, the result of bold Soviet action in Yugoslavia would be to "Austrianize" Italy (under whatever leadership subsequently might emerge in Rome, whether leftist or not).

Certainly the military implications for Italy of Soviet military bases in Yugoslavia would be considerable. Probably the most vulnerable section of Italy consists of the 50-kilometer-wide Gorizia Gap on the Italian northeastern border opposite Slovenia. It was in this region that the bloody battle of Caporetto was fought in 1917. An attacking force breaking through the gap would find itself in the easily traversable plains of northeastern Italy. Within this region lies the vital industrial triangle formed by Milan, Bologna, and Venice. Such an attack through the Gorizia Gap could be augmented by airborne strikes from Soviet air bases in Yugoslavia, just across the narrow Adriatic. Moreover, the Italian communications network on the eastern coast is highly vulnerable because of the Appennine Mountains, which restrict major lines of communication essentially to a thin coastal route running from Taranto to Bologna. Thus, a Soviet airborne and/or amphibious venture launched across the Adriatic easily could sever Italian north-south communications, thereby facilitating the fall of northern Italy.

Moreover, recent military reorganization, necessitated by economic problems, has reduced the number of brigades in the Italian army from 36 to 24. This factor, in addition to "promotional laws" requiring that a major part of Italian military hardware be procured domestically—a provision also brought about by relative economic hardship within Italy (and, in a sense, probably by the desire to preempt part of the appeal of the PCI to voters suffering from economic deprivation)—may have undermined considerably Italy's ability to defend itself against a significant Warsaw Pact force along its border. Thus, Rome—finding itself confronted by superior Soviet power, painfully aware of Italy's ideologically divided society, and perhaps viewing NATO's credibility as dwindling—simply might give in to Soviet pressures.

An argument certainly can be made to the effect that daring Soviet moves in Yugoslavia, if not counteracted psychologically by dramatic Western reactions, might create the perception that NATO, and the United States in particular, could not be relied upon to rescue beleaguered clients. Such an impression might reflect the cumulative impact of perceived Soviet victories in the face of varying degrees of Western impotence—in Czechoslovakia, 1968; Vietnam, Laos, Cambodia; the 1973 Middle Eastern War; and Angola, followed by Yugoslavia. That is not to say that states observing this phenomenon would become fonder of the Soviet Union; however, they might become more respectful of Soviet power and of the Soviet will and determination to use that power, in contrast to a "decaying" Western empire unwilling or unable to assert itself. The implication of such perceptions well might be that disengagement from the NATO alliance and a search for accommodation with Moscow, while distasteful, might be viewed as pragmatically necessary.

Greece and Turkey

If Italy might be intimidated into disengagement from NATO by bold Soviet action in the Balkans, then Greece

should have even more incentive to follow suit.[20] The Greeks
long have confronted a hostile Bulgarian border to the north.
However, despite their nominally Communist status, the
Yugoslav and Albanian regimes have not cooperated with the
Bulgars in any anti-Greek ventures since 1948. If Yugoslavia
were to fall under Soviet influence—an event that could lead to
an alteration in the status and allegiance of Albania—Greece
might find itself, barely a generation after the events leading to
the promulgation of the Truman Doctrine, facing, on three
fronts, states under Soviet influence—all seeking to topple
Greek democracy.

While a Warsaw Pact penetration along the Greco-
Bulgarian border, through the Struma Valley, and into the
center of Greek Macedonia, already looms as a possibility
worthy of Greek consideration, Soviet control of southern
Yugoslavia could complicate considerably the protection of
Greece against a potential Warsaw Pact attacking force. It
should be noted that the mountain passes along the Bulgarian
border essentially run from east to west and thus could be more
easily defended against an attacking force from the north
(presumably attempting to break through to the Aegean Sea,
some 80 kilometers to the south) than could be the north to
south mountain passes found just south of Greece's border
with Yugoslavia.

Two natural invasion routes lead from Yugoslavia into
Greece (in addition to the Struma route), both of which were
utilized by the attacking German Twelfth Army during 1941:
the Monastir-Florina and Vardar gaps, leading to the Axios-
Aliakmon Valley to the west of Thessaloniki (Salonika). The
Vardar corridor, the eastern gap, provides an ideal funnel for
an invader toward the Thermïkos Kolpos (the Gulf of
Salonika), which is only about 75 kilometers from the point
where the Vardar River enters Greece. By capturing the Axios-
Aliakmon Valley, an invading force could drive a wedge into

northern Greece, cutting off the bulk of the country from the northeastern panhandle, which consists of Thrace and eastern Macedonia and includes the important port of Thessaloniki (the second largest city in Greece, with a population close to 350,000 and of growing industrial significance). The Struma route, by contrast, leads to points to the east of Thessaloniki and thus would require a sharp westward swing by invading forces seeking to cordon off this important area of Greece. In order to redress the military asymmetry in favor of the Warsaw Pact along the northern border of Greece, the West would be required to redeploy forces significantly, at a time when the political climate favors large cutbacks (see Appendix 6).

The possibility that Soviet control over Yugoslavia would be extended to Albania means that still a third Warsaw Pact base could be established for attack on Greece. However, the military significance of adding Soviet bases in Albania to those in Bulgaria and Yugoslavia would be marginal, at least in terms of potential land and air attacks. That the geography of the region is rugged was demonstrated by the major difficulties encountered during the ultimately unsuccessful Italian offensive against Greece in 1940-41, which stalled in the formidable Pindus Mountains, with the invaders finally being pushed back into Albanian territory.

Nevertheless, the psychological implications if Greece were confronted on three fronts by Soviet allies or satellites might be significant—particularly since, in the case of the Yugoslav and, to a lesser degree, Bulgarian invasion routes, the military ramifications of Soviet pressure might prove irresistible. The Greco-Bulgarian border is about 400 kilometers long; Greece's frontiers with Albania and Yugoslavia measure some 280 kilometers each. Thus, the extension of Soviet power to Yugoslavia would increase the length of Greece's land borders with Soviet-dominated regions by about 70 percent, while Soviet control of both Yugoslavia and Albania would increase the length of the frontier by 140 percent. Certainly such statistics would have to have a psychological effect on Greece.

This is likely to be the case particularly since Greece's only other neighbor is Turkey, a country which has been hostile to Greece throughout much of this and the previous century. Not only does the Greek state share a 200-kilometer-long land boundary with Turkey, it confronts the Turkish mainland along many hundreds of kilometers of the Aegean Sea—a focal point of Greek vulnerability being the Dodecanese Islands, located within a few kilometers of the Turkish coast.[21] Thus the extension of Soviet dominance over another or possibly two more of Greece's northern neighbors might be viewed in Athens as requiring desperate measures.

So far, the NATO framework has not succeeded in satisfying Greek demands with regard to the Greek-Turkish dispute. The Greek government has been antagonized to such an extent that in 1975 it refused to allow maneuvers under the NATO designation "Operation Deep Express" to be conducted on Greek territory, unless all Turkish forces were prevented from participating in such joint operations. Since "Operation Deep Express" was designed to thwart the contingency of a thrust (presumably by the Warsaw Pact) into Greek Thrace from Bulgaria, it would seem to follow that the Greek government is concerned more about Turkey than about a Communist incursion into Greece. However, if the Soviet Union were to gain a toehold in Yugoslavia and perhaps in Albania as well, the Greek government might have to shift its focus away from the Turkish conflict and toward a Soviet-backed threat; such a shift would imply patching up the long-standing quarrel with Turkey and reentering NATO in a full capacity. On the other hand, if the Greeks were to retain their traditional preoccupation with Turkey, even after Soviet or Warsaw Pact actions at the expense of the sovereignty of Greece's northern neighbors, the Greek government might be tempted eventually to tilt toward the Warsaw Pact.

Warsaw Pact successes in the Balkans, coming in the wake of other Soviet victories, might be viewed as indicative of overall NATO or American weakness, either objective or subjective. Moreover, while the United States and other NATO powers cannot with any credibility promise to back Greece unconditionally against Turkey (another NATO ally) the Soviet Union would not find itself so constrained. Thus, if Greece suddenly found itself surrounded by Soviet-dominated states as a result of a display of apparent Soviet strength and corresponding American weakness in the region, the Greek government might be tempted to disengage from a demonstrably weak southern flank of NATO. Athens then might be prepared to entertain any offers that might emanate from a Moscow regime which, however unpalatable, seemed firmly to be in control of the destiny of the region.

In this connection, it must be remembered that, despite the bitter experiences that the "cradle of democracy" encountered with communism in the period immediately after World War II, the Greek state may not be imbued with inveterate antipathy toward Russia. After all, for centuries there has been a tie between the Russian and Greek Orthodox churches, and a corresponding similarity between the two alphabets. Moreover, as students of Greek history must be aware, Russian intervention against Turkey during the Greek war of independence was instrumental in Greece's attainment of freedom. Thus, while the bulk of the Greek people may have severe doubts about communism or the present Soviet regime, there is a historical basis for Russo-Greek cooperation.

In the same manner that a show of Soviet strength in the Balkans might have either of two basically incompatible long-term effects on Athens, it would have the potential to cause either of two opposing political developments in Ankara. On the one hand, the Turkish government might be alarmed sufficiently by such an event to move it toward compromise on such salient differences with the Greeks as the future of Aegean oil, fortification of Aegean Islands, and the Cyprus problem, in order to promote a resurgence of NATO's southern flank in the face of the increased Warsaw Pact threat. However, an entirely different reaction by the Ankara government is also possible. It is conceivable that Turkey might be so disappointed at the inability of the West to sustain the essentially neutral status of the Yugoslav state that Ankara might begin to slide politically toward the Soviet Union.

While it is true that, in view of Greece's propinquity to the Yugoslav state, Athens would be more likely than the Turkish government to react strongly to Soviet activities in the Balkans, it is equally the case that Turkey shares a long border with the Soviet Union, and thus must remain sensitive to Soviet displays of power. Moreover (although, unlike the Greeks, the Turks have not withdrawn their military forces from NATO), it would be logical to assume a considerable degree of Turkish resentment towards the West, in view of the arms embargo imposed on Turkey by the U.S. Congress after the 1974 Greek-Turkish conflict over Cyprus. One must also bear in mind historical precedents of Turkish cooperation with the USSR. As has been well documented, the Turkish national hero Kemal Atatürk formed an alliance with the Soviet Union in 1920 which included the shipment of arms to Turkey. The military aid received from the USSR enabled the Turks, after several victorious battles, to recover (at the 1922 Lausanne peace settlement) large amounts of territory lost to the Greeks under the first postwar settlement, at Sèvres, imposed on Turkey by the Allies.[22] Perhaps Turkey might be tempted to recreate the circumstances that led to its successes at the expense of Greece prior to Lausanne.

While it seems most unlikely that the Soviet Union could succeed in detaching both Greece and Turkey from NATO because of the antipathy between the two "allies," it is possible that the Soviet leaders might be able to offer one of the two governments sufficient inducements to withdraw from the Western alliance, which must maintain an "evenhanded" policy toward its two partners.

Austria

Another state which might be affected psychologically by events in Yugoslavia is Austria. A nominally neutral state, Austria provides a corridor for Western access to Hungary, as well as a border with Yugoslavia and Czechoslovakia. If the Soviet Union were able to "Finlandize" Austria, it could thereby insulate the satellite states from the West, to an even greater degree than at present.

In summation, it would appear that, while rash Soviet action in Yugoslavia (and perhaps subsequently in Albania) might present pitfalls for the USSR, the potential harm to Soviet interests is unlikely to offset the tangible strategic gains to be made from acquiring bases in Yugoslavia and, possibly, Albania. While the initial reaction of Western-oriented states in the region might be to coalesce around NATO in an attempt to forestall further Soviet gains, the longer-term reactions of at least some of the governments concerned might be to move away from an ineffective southern NATO flank, particularly if the USSR were to offer some tangible inducements for doing so.

7

The Military Implications of a Change in the Status Quo

In geostrategic terms, Yugoslavia is of profound military importance within the context of the NATO–Warsaw Pact confrontation in Europe. Bordering on such non–Warsaw Pact countries as Greece, Italy, Austria, and Albania, with a long coastline on the Adriatic Sea (which opens into the center of the Mediterranean), Yugoslavia is nestled in the heart of NATO's southern flank. Thus, should the Soviet Union acquire hegemony over the Yugoslav state, the USSR could gain a high degree of influence over the evolution of Eastern Mediterranean politics, not only with regard to Southern and Central Europe, but also vis-à-vis North Africa and the Middle East (with its increasingly visible symbolic importance, as well as its objective value in terms of important natural resources). Moreover, domination over Yugoslavia would offer the Soviet Union a frontier with Albania, a recalcitrant former satellite that long has proved an embarrassment to the USSR.

In terms of access to the Mediterranean, Yugoslav ports

offer the Soviet leaders an opportunity to overcome Russia's traditional problem of constraints resulting from foreign control both of the numerous islands which dominate the Aegean Sea and of the straits of the Dardanelles and the Bosphorus. To this day, at least legally, the Soviet Union is limited in its passage through the straits by the July 1936 Montreux Convention regarding the regime of the straits, which was signed by Great Britain, Bulgaria, France, Greece, Japan, Romania, Turkey, the USSR, and Yugoslavia.[1] This agreement placed heavy restrictions on the passage of warships through the straits, in wartime and in peacetime, by Black Sea powers as well as non–Black Sea powers. The expanded Soviet presence in the Mediterranean during the past several years undoubtedly has increased the importance of unhampered entry into that sea from the waters of the Warsaw Pact states. The Soviet navy, which, in recent times, has maintained a "Mediterranean Eskadra" consisting of about forty-five vessels, has invested high stakes in the region.[2] Moscow certainly wishes to insure the operational capability of its vessels—a goal that might be realized more easily through increased availability of docking, repair, and reload facilities and easy access for auxiliary vessels. Moreover, should a superpower confrontation ever degenerate into a direct military conflict between East and West in the Mediterranean, the Russians would wish to have readily available reinforcements for the Soviet Mediterranean squadron. The Soviet Union during the 1970s has maintained a naval presence of approximately eighty combat vessels in the Black Sea (including about forty surface combat vessels, in addition to some forty submarines).[3] Obviously it would be useful for the Soviet leadership to be able to transfer at least part of the Black Sea Fleet to the Mediterranean, unhampered, in order to tip the scales against the U.S. Sixth Fleet.

In this context, the Montreux Convention poses significant difficulties. Specifically, Article 12 normally prohibits passage of submarines into the Mediterranean, while the fourteenth article provides that during peacetime a maximum aggregate of 15,000 tons, representing at most nine vessels, may be sent at one time through the Turkish Straits.[4] Article 11 allows the Black Sea riparians to overshoot the 15,000-ton limit, but only in the event that a "capital ship" (i.e., a battleship that displaces more than 10,000 tons) comprises the bulk of the weight; in that case, at most one such ship may traverse the straits at one time, and it may be escorted by no more than two destroyers. Thus, the Soviet Union may, at any given time, send through the Black Sea egress no more than one guided-missile cruiser or one *Moskva*-class antisubmarine warfare helicopter carrier "cruiser," accompanied by two destroyers.[5] Furthermore, Article 13 specifies that any ships passing through the straits must be registered eight days in advance with the proper Turkish authorities, along with a listing of the precise destination, type and number of vessels, and, if requested, notification of the intended date of return. Similarly, Article 23 requires that three days' notice be given to Turkey prior to overflight of the straits by civil aircraft.[6] However, there have been persistent reports of overflight of other portions of Turkish territory (e.g., Anatolia) by Soviet civil and military aircraft on their way to Syria.

Perhaps more objectionable from the Soviet standpoint is the absolute restriction placed (in Article 19) upon passage of warships of belligerents through the Turkish straits, except in the context of mutual assistance pacts concluded under League of Nations (subsequently United Nations) auspices to assist victims of aggression.[7] In fact, Turkey has not been very strict in its enforcement of this provision, choosing not to close the straits to belligerents in what the Arab states consider to be an ongoing war with Israel.

Actually, in the modern era, the whole concept of "war" has become obfuscated. Is the Cold War a war? Are guerrilla wars war? Is the Arab interpretation of the long-term conflict with Israel—as constituting one prolonged war—correct? Obviously, there is ample room for a high degree of subjective interpretation in such cases. The Soviet Union probably feels that it could not rely with absolute certainty upon favorable Turkish interpretations during strategically important moments.

Thus an unfavorable provision from the Soviet standpoint is Article 20, which provides that interpretations concerning passage of warships be left entirely to the discretion of the Turkish government. Moreover, the following article provides for implementation of Article 20 whenever Turkey should consider herself in "imminent danger of war."[8] According to Article 21 (at least theoretically) Turkey may temporarily lock up a portion of the Soviet fleet in the Black Sea, thus stranding a section of the Soviet navy in the Mediterranean, cut off from its Black Sea bases. This provision infuriated Stalin in 1945, when he stated that the article had created an "impossible situation," since according to its stipulations, "a small state backed by Great Britain held a great state by the throat and gave it no outlet."[9]

Even without the disadvantages contained in Articles 20 and 21, the Soviet Union could be severely hampered by the Montreux Convention. As noted earlier, submarines may not pass through the Dardanelles (except for damaged vessels which have to travel on the surface—thereby exposing their position and thus vitiating the major advantage of the submarine, namely, the ability of keep its position hidden). Consequently, in order to enter the Mediterranean from bases within the Soviet Union or to return to secure homeland bases, during times of crisis Soviet submarines must circumnavigate Europe, a distance of more than 4,000 miles.[10] In so doing, they must pass through areas likely to be patrolled by NATO antisubmarine warfare (ASW) vessels, including a NATO "chokepoint" (either in the Spitsbergen-Norway gap or the even slimmer Kattegat and the adjacent narrows of the Belt between Denmark and Sweden). Moreover, the Montreux Convention's requirement of prior notice for transit through the Dardanelles, together with its limitation of the number of ships and/or amount of tonnage allowed to traverse the straits at any one time, can result in lengthening the "spill-out" period needed to move the bulk of the Soviet Black Sea fleet into the Mediterranean to between thirty and forty days.[11] Without the legal constraints of the Montreux Convention, this process would take considerably less time; large-scale reinforcements for the Mediterranean squadron probably could arrive within three or four days of being requested.

The Soviet Union has been able, intermittently, to obtain Mediterranean shore facilities—however, never with the degree of certainty considered desirable by Russian leaders seeking to guarantee a secure Mediterranean presence. In 1958 the Soviet navy obtained a base at Valona, Albania. However, when the Soviet-Albanian rift occurred in 1961, the Albanians terminated Soviet privileges at the strategically located port, which at that time was servicing eight Soviet W-class submarines and two Russian submarine tenders. In response, the Kremlin unceremoniously lowered the Albanian flag on vessels already transferred to the Albanian navy and sailed them back to Soviet ports.

Subsequent to that period, major full-time Soviet facilities in the Mediterranean were located in Egypt—in Alexandria and Port Said since October 7, 1967, and in Mersa Matruh since 1968 (according to a five-year agreement renewed in 1973).[12] During this period, the Soviet navy increasingly has utilized also the Syrian port of Latakia. Although since the alleged Soviet-Egyptian "rift" there appears to have been a diminution in Soviet use of Egyptian facilities (at least at Alexandria and Port Said), the shift of Soviet emphasis to Latakia also may reflect the superior location of the Syrian facilities, from the

Soviet standpoint—well to the north of the Egyptian bases and closer to the Black Sea.

The Soviet navy, moreover, has increased quietly its utilization of Yugoslav ports. In fact, in 1975, Yugoslavia changed its ports rights regulations, enabling a Soviet submarine tender and a Soviet submarine to complete repairs in Tivat. Late in that year, the Russians installed a floating drydock in the port, thereby enhancing their capacity to support the Soviet Mediterranean Fleet.[13] From the Soviet perspective, the Adriatic probably is the ideal spot for a naval base: it is most useful for the Russians to have a way-station to the Middle East, so that in the event of conflict, the Soviet Union can resupply its clients without having to traverse the straits, particularly given the restrictions stemming from the Montreux Convention.

In fact, during the 1973 war, the USSR did use the Yugoslav port of Rijeka as an embarkation point for sealifting heavy equipment, including T-54 tanks, to the Middle East. By establishing a land link from Hungary to Rijeka, the Russians were able to dispatch 60,000 tons of materiel per week to Egypt and Syria. During the years immediately preceding the 1975 arrangements, the Soviet navy had been paying a great many visits to Yugoslavia, docking at Rijeka, Split, Kotor, Dubrovnik, Hercegnovi, and Tivat.[14]

While the Kremlin must be pleased to have some Soviet naval facilities on the Dalmatian coast, the history of Soviet-Yugoslav relations appears to indicate that such privileges cannot be relied upon as long as Tito—or presumably, a successor "Titoist" regime—maintains power. Should the Soviet Union gain hegemony over post-Tito Yugoslavia, it would be in a position to maintain secure port facilities with direct land links to Warsaw Pact territory and with relatively free access to the Mediterranean. Not only would such a development safeguard Soviet sealift and airlift operations to the Middle East and other potential crisis spots in the Mediterranean region, it would enhance greatly a Soviet war-waging capacity in the area. Apart from the ability to bring reinforcements rapidly to the scene of a local conflict, the Soviet navy would have relatively safe bases at which to service its vessels during battle. Soviet facilities in the Middle East—irrespective of whether they may be considered dependable (remembering the volatility and instability of the Middle Eastern regimes in question)—could not be regarded as entirely secure during major conflicts, in view of the propinquity of the generally effective Israeli Air Force. This consideration would have to be kept in mind, since a confrontation in the Mediterranean well might be an offshoot of the Arab-Israeli conflict.

These factors, in addition to the location of the Yugoslav coast—near the center of the Mediterranean, and thus within relatively short sail of any potential Mediterranean conflict—must render Yugoslav ports extremely desirable from the Soviet point of view. Perhaps the most important function such ports could serve would be to provide the Soviet navy with facilities for reloading its Kara-class, Kresta I–class, and Kresta II–class guided-missile cruisers, none of which are thought to possess on-board reload capacities for their Shaddock ship-to-ship cruise missiles.[15] Thus, during a Warsaw Pact–NATO naval conflict, a centrally located, Soviet-controlled port could prove invaluable to the Russian navy, enabling it to take fullest advantage of its anti-ship-warfare capability.

Perhaps no less important for the Warsaw Pact than acquisition of directly controlled naval access to the Mediterranean would be the extension of its air coverage over that sea. At present, the Warsaw Pact does not control direct air access to the central sector of the Mediterranean, except intermittently, e.g., when granted overflight privileges by the Yugoslavs (such as permission to resupply Russia's clients in Angola in 1976 and the Soviet Union's Syrian and Egyptian friends during the

Yom Kippur War in 1973).[16] Tacitly, Turkey too has chosen
not to interfere with Warsaw Pact air traffic to Soviet facilities
in the Middle East.[17]

Russian facilities in Syria, as well as the much more restrict-
ed access that the Egyptians still may be allowing the USSR,
could provide Soviet pilots with bases from which to fly
combat and tracking missions (as opposed to overflight of
Yugoslavia or Turkey, which presumably could be utilized
only for logistical resupply missions under present circumstances). However, facilities in these Arab countries are located too
far east to allow Russian air combat missions over the *central*
or *western* sectors of the Mediterranean, given the limited
combat radii of Soviet tactical aircraft.[18] Thus, the Warsaw
Pact cannot at present adequately control by air the major
strategic choke point of the Sicilian Channel, between Sicily
and Tunisia, over 800 miles from Alexandria and 1,200 miles
from Latakia. Soviet air bases in Yugoslavia would be located
between 500 and 550 miles from that channel, well within the
range of Soviet tactical aircraft. Control of this vital region by
Soviet air and sea forces could enable the USSR, during a
crisis, to seal off the U.S. Sixth Fleet from the eastern Mediterranean, thereby endangering Israel and significantly increasing
Soviet pressure on Greece and Turkey (see Appendix 7).

In fact, bases in Yugoslavia not only might enable Warsaw
Pact forces to seal off the eastern Mediterranean and dominate
the central sector of that sea, but also would give the USSR
significant capability to influence events in the western Mediterranean, through resort to some of the longer-range Soviet
aircraft. While at present only the newly deployed Soviet
Backfire-B bomber has the range, on a return mission, to hit
the westernmost U.S. base in the Mediterranean (at Rota,
Spain), the old Tu-16 Badger, flying out of Adriatic bases,
could cover the entire area up to Rota on a return basis.
Moreover, many of the tactical aircraft mentioned earlier, as

well as the Tu-22 Blinder bomber, could reach Rota on a one-way mission from bases in Yugoslavia if necessary (and certainly could fly return missions in seas immediately to the west of Italy).

Similarly, the surveillance capacity of the USSR would be extended considerably, since the major reconnaissance aircraft in the Soviet arsenal (with the phasing out of the old propeller-driven Tu-95) are likely to be reconnaissance versions of the Tu-16 and the MiG-25, which are subject to the same range limitations as the combat versions.[19] Warsaw Pact control of airfields within reach of the central and western Mediterranean is important particularly in terms of Soviet antisubmarine warfare (ASW) capacity and of Russian capability to eliminate NATO surface vessels. This is of special significance for a country like the Soviet Union which lacks major ocean-based naval air forces, and thus must rely heavily upon shore-based aircraft. The Soviet navy deploys a force of some 650 shore-based combat aircraft, including 280 Tu-16 Badger medium bombers armed with air-to-surface missiles (Kennel or Kelt), 30 newly deployed Backfire-B medium bombers (also armed with ASMs), and 60 Tu-22 Blinder medium bombers, as well as light bombers, assorted transport planes, tankers, and reconnaissance aircraft. In addition, the USSR deploys a large number of ASW aircraft, including some 250 Mi-4 Hound and Ka-25 Hormone ASW helicopters, about 55 K-38 May ASW patrol planes (the Soviet equivalent of the American P-3 Orion), and other ASW airplanes, including some Bear-Fs which have been adapted for ASW use. Each of the new *Kiev*-class carriers has only about 25 V/STOL plus helicopters on board, and the two *Moskva*-class ASW helicopter cruisers carry no fixed-wing aircraft.[20] Under these circumstances, the Soviet naval air force clearly can be effective against U.S. attack carrier forces equipped with ultra-modern fighters only if the generally slow Russian attack planes can be protected by tactical squadrons of the Soviet air force. However, in view of the limited combat radii of the latter, as this analysis has pointed out, extending such protection would require air bases in proximity to the central Mediterranean—such as on the Dalmatian Coast.

According to some interpretations, the basic emphasis of Soviet naval battle doctrine, as it has developed in recent years, has been upon coordination of cruise missile ships with air-, sea-, and satellite-based surveillance; the intention is to overwhelm Western naval defenses in a swift surprise attack, together with a land offensive in the case of a major Mediterranean regional confrontation. Thus, according to one authority, "the key to success is obtaining constant up-to-date target information—the requirement is, therefore, very highclass surveillance of enemy units."[21] In such a scenario, a surprise attack in the Mediterranean would be utilized for seizing control of Western sea lines of communications (SLOC). The attainment of this objective obviously would prove fatal to NATO defenses during a prolonged battle, particularly since the Soviet Union maintains direct land links with the heart of Central Europe, while the United States must traverse the Atlantic in order to reinforce NATO troops. Such a Soviet surprise attack also would enable the Russians to deprive NATO defenses of aircraft carrier–based air coverage—an important component of what some regard as an increasingly questionable NATO capability to defend itself against potential Warsaw Pact thrusts aimed at the vulnerable flanks of the Western alliance.[22] Control of secure bases in the Mediterranean would increase Soviet chances of launching a successful surprise attack against Sixth Fleet forces. First, availability of such bases probably would enable the Russians to increase the number of full-time tracking vessels (the so-called auxiliary general intelligence ships, or AGIs) on call in the Mediterranean, thus improving their capability to cover the Sixth Fleet.[23]

Second, once in possession of these bases, the Soviet Union could avoid having to send its ships through the Gibraltar and Dardanelles "choke points," thereby complicating NATO surveillance tasks. This would increase the likelihood that the NATO command might lack adequate warnings about a Soviet buildup in the Mediterranean, and thus might not be fully prepared for a Soviet surprise attack.

Not only would Soviet hegemony over Yugoslavia enable the USSR to gain important Yugoslav bases, but Soviet control of Yugoslavia might well be exploited by the Russians, or by forces favorable to them, to bring about a shift in Albania's political position—which, of course, for some time has been militantly anti-Soviet. Were the Soviet Union to increase its political influence in Albania, it would seek to regain its basing rights in Valona, near the mouth of the Adriatic. Soviet bases in Albania would place the Soviet navy closer still to the central Mediterranean and guarantee Soviet control of the eastern portion of the Straits of Otranto, at the mouth of the Adriatic—thus rendering it extremely difficult for the NATO allies to close off the Adriatic during a war. (If Russia controlled bases in Yugoslavia but not in Albania, the Soviet navy conceivably might be bottled up in the Adriatic.)

8

Scenarios of Foreign Intervention

The ability of the Yugoslav state to defend itself against foreign incursion is beset by complex problems, the solution of which entails various factors that transcend strictly military affairs; matters of international politics and Yugoslav domestic affairs undoubtedly merit consideration in this context.[1]

Military power, of course, is a relative concept and must be analyzed, therefore, in a comparative manner. At this juncture, Yugoslavia's potential adversaries would appear to be comprised of various permutations of Bulgarian, Soviet, and, conceivably, Albanian forces, with the likelihood that Soviet involvement would entail also the use of contingents from other Warsaw Pact members.

Bulgarian and/or Albanian intervention probably would arise in connection with irredentist claims. Soviet involvement is likely to be based on strategic, ideological, and hegemonic considerations. Yugoslavia is of major strategic significance in the present constellation of power: Soviet control of the Yugoslav Adriatic coast would enable the USSR practically to cut in half NATO's Southern Command—jeopardizing Italy's security, compelling a shift in concentration of Western forces from the Ionian and Tyrrhenian seas to the Adriatic, and adding an "incalculable element to the Italian political equation."[2] Moreover, the emplacement of NATO air and sea bases on the Adriatic, by requiring a move northward, would create gaps in the Western defense system further south, in the central and eastern Mediterranean. This would enable the Soviet Union considerably to enhance its position in the Middle East and (by increasing Soviet capabilities to interfere with U.S. Sixth Fleet operations in the Eastern Mediterranean) possibly could open the way for the Russians to impose a naval blockade on Israel.[3]

The ability of the Yugoslav state to withstand foreign intervention could be undermined by any of several potentially subversive elements. In addition to being hampered probably by a power struggle for the succession, based on nonideological factors, Yugoslavia might well be undermined by the so-called "Cominformists," a pro-Soviet faction; by various dissatisfied ethnic groups, particularly the Croats; and by separatist groups among the Albanians, Macedonians, or the Hungarians. Indeed, even the loyalty of the liberal so-called *Praxis* faction might be suspect—although, as a self-proclaimed purist Titoist group, it probably could be counted on to oppose any anti-Titoist incursion.

The most likely scenario for intervention would postulate an indigenous force, alone or aided by emigrés, initiating turmoil, perhaps even an uprising, and then proceeding to "invite in" aid from abroad. This could take the form of Kosmet Albanians requesting Tirana's help, Macedonians asking for Sofia's assistance, or, perhaps, "Cominformists," or even Croat nationalists, "inviting" Soviet aid. If no such requests were genuinely forthcoming, however, "invitations" could be fabricated and used as a pretext for intervention, as was demonstrated by the Soviet Union during the 1968 invasion of

Czechoslovakia. Precisely in anticipation of such a development, Yugoslavia included in its 1970 Federal Defense Law the following provision:

> No one has the right to invite the enemy's armed forces into the country and to help enemies carry out any type of forcible measure toward our citizens and to collaborate with them in the political and economic field.[4]

Intervention by Western forces in favor of the Yugoslav central government probably could not be counted on with any certainty, for a number of reasons: First, recent events in Angola would appear to indicate that the United States (or, at least, Congress) is reluctant to take a firm stand abroad after the debacle in Vietnam, probably with the exception of responding to an attack upon NATO territory. In the second place, the southern flank of NATO appears to be in a process of gradual dissolution, due to quarrels both with Greece and Turkey regarding American policy during the 1974 Cyprus crisis (although negotiations are continuing with Athens and Ankara concerning military facilities and future coordination with NATO).

In recent years, Yugoslavia's most friendly neighbor tended to be Romania. After the invasion of Prague, the two countries cooperated quite closely on military, diplomatic, and economic affairs.[5] Presumably the two "renegade" socialist states found it valuable to present a united front of sorts vis-à-vis a Soviet leadership that was feared to be considering armed intervention. Examples of this cooperation included joint development of the "Eagle" (*"Orao"*), a fairly sophisticated jet interceptor aircraft, and the Iron Gates Dam project on the Danube.[6] The Yugoslavs also issued numerous statements implying that the friendship between the two countries was based on the need to maintain their independence in the face of Soviet hegemonic aspirations. Typical of this view was the declaration made by Romania's foreign minister, Georghe Macovescu, that relations with Yugoslavia are founded

> on mutual respect and confidence, on the respect of their independence and national sovereignty, non-interference in internal affairs, equality, mutual benefit, solidarity and comradely mutual help.[7]

However, both the ability and the willingness of the Romanians actually to embroil themselves in an armed conflict on behalf of another state, even Yugoslavia, would have to be questioned seriously. The Romanian policy of presenting the appearance of a united front with Yugoslavia probably is predicated on the hope of deterring the Soviet leadership from intervening directly in Romania. Thus, it is doubtful that the Romanians voluntarily would choose to become involved in a conflict which would place them in confrontation with the Russian army. Moreover, Romania's ability to turn the tide, were the Yugoslavs forced into armed combat with the USSR, is questionable indeed.

In fact, Yugoslavia and Romania already may be encountering some difficulties. Certainly Belgrade must be unhappy at the apparent improvement in relations between Romania and Bulgaria, as symbolized by Ceauşescu's summer-of-1976 visit to Varna for the purpose of holding talks with Zhivkov.[8] The Romanians have been moving not only toward the Bulgarians but apparently also toward the Soviet Union—not surprisingly, since it is rare indeed to find Sofia pursuing any line independent of Moscow. When Brezhnev visited Ceauşescu in November 1976, the Soviet leader emphasized that by "perfecting the division of labor among the socialist countries, we can provide extremely vast outlets for the national industry of each fraternal country."[9] This statement implied not only an increase in trade between the two states but also specialization by each in the production, respectively, of raw materials and manufactured goods within a closely integrated Comecon network. This "division of labor," if implemented, once again would place such less developed East European countries as Romania in the position of being little more than quasi-colonies of the USSR and of the more industrial East European states, particularly Czechoslovakia, East Germany, and Poland. It was precisely over this question that Ceauşescu's predecessor first fell out with the Kremlin well over a decade ago, in Khrushchev's days, and moved Romania into a position of demonstrative autonomy vis-à-vis the USSR, the Warsaw Pact, and Comecon. Thus, "socialist division of labor" in this context is a code phrase for subordinating Romania once more to Moscow's hegemony.

It is significant, moreover, that the Romanians unexpectedly made a major concession to the USSR on the issue of Moldavia, after prolonged disagreement with the Kremlin over this question. Despite long-term Chinese incitement of Romania over the Soviet seizure of Moldavia in World War II, Ceauşescu, on June 2, 1976, informed a cultural congress that Romania had "no territorial or other problems with the Soviet Union or other neighboring socialist countries." Soon afterward, in an unprecedented step for a Romanian leader, he visited the Moldavian SSR; at the same time, however, he toured also two additional Soviet republics, thereby implying that he viewed Moldavia simply as another Soviet republic.[10] Moreover, in what cannot be regarded as an insignificant event, when visiting Moscow in August 1976 Ceauşescu adopted the Soviet position concerning the need for "proletarian internationalism."[11] That term was highly reminiscent of the language of the Brezhnev Doctrine which Belgrade has opposed violently in the past; consequently, the joint conference document issued by the 1976 East Berlin Conference of European Communist

Parties specifically omitted this phrase in favor of a more neutral reference to "internationalist, comradely and voluntary co-operation and solidarity, on the basis of the great ideas of Marx, Engels and Lenin."[12] Thus, on a major ideological point, the Romanians apparently have sided with the USSR.

To be sure, Bucharest, on its part, has had cause to feel that Tito may have "sold out" to Moscow (see Chapter 9), and there seems to be no way at present to establish just who has been "letting down" whom. It may be significant also, if only symbolically, that the jointly produced *"Orao"* fighter plane lately has encountered what the Western press has been informed are "technical complications." Assuming that the difficulties in fact are merely technical, the inability of the two states to manufacture a plane without difficulty, after years of cooperation, may indicate to the two regimes the futility of attempting to resist Soviet hegemonism, given the contradictions between and within Yugoslavia and Romania.[13]

The relative levels of materiel in the possession of the Yugoslav, Bulgarian, and Albanian armed forces would seem to indicate that, under any but the most unfavorable circumstances, the Yugoslav military apparatus would have comparatively little trouble repelling an attack by either or even both of its two potentially most hostile neighbors; this may be assumed particularly since the prospective areas of combat cover mountainous, easily defensible terrain. In the light of this factor, it is difficult to comprehend why Tito has seen fit to start building new roads linking the center of Macedonia with previously inaccessible frontier areas near Bulgaria and Albania respectively, thus easing the task of prospective invaders.

The most modern combat planes of the Yugoslav air force include 110 MiG-21 F/PFs, as compared to altogether only 48 MiG-21s and the older and rather unreliable MiG-19s, and Chinese versions of these two planes (the F-8s and F-6s respectively), possessed by the Albanians, and 84 MiG-21s and

MiG-19s comprising the combat squadrons of the Bulgarian air force. The Yugoslav heavy and medium tank corps is composed of 1,500 T-54s, T-34s, and M-47s, as well as 650 M-4s—a force that is roughly comparable in size and quality to Bulgaria's armored forces, which consist of some 2,000 T-54/55s and T-34s (although, ominously, they include also the first T-62s to be deployed in that country), but vastly superior to Albania's, which can field only about 140 comparable tanks, mostly of obsolescent vintage. Nor is Yugoslavia lacking in military manpower, with regular forces of about 250,000 men (backed by 500,000 reservists and 600,000 men of the local militias—the Territorial Defense Forces). By comparison, Bulgaria has regular forces of some 165,000 men only, with some 285,000 reservists and a 150,000-man-strong "People's Militia," and Albania has a mere 47,000 regulars, plus some 100,000 reservists. None of the three countries possesses a major naval capability.[14]

However, the most likely scenario for a military confrontation involving Yugoslavia presents contingencies other than isolated armed conflict with Bulgaria or Albania individually. As explained in Chapter 1, the most likely Bulgarian attack upon Yugoslavia would be launched, not in isolation, but jointly with the Soviet Union. (Needless to say, Yugoslavia would be most unlikely to attack Bulgaria, as long as the latter is allied closely with the USSR.) As for the Albanians, they are unlikely to make a military move of their own, recently renewed polemics notwithstanding, both for the political reasons mentioned, and because of marked military inferiority. The Yugoslavs are equally unlikely to attack Albania, since such an adventure would leave them politically and militarily vulnerable to a Soviet/Warsaw Pact–aided attack by Bulgaria. The real threat, therefore, to the security of the area emanates from the possibility of a coordinated Warsaw Pact military intervention in Yugoslavia—supplemented, perhaps, by the incursions of nationalist and other emigrés and by nationalist uprisings within the country itself.

Before discussing the purely military-strategic position of Yugoslavia vis-à-vis the Warsaw Pact forces, it is necessary to analyze weaknesses inherent in the Yugoslav defense network. The army could well be viewed by dissident nationalists as essentially a tool of the Serbs. No less than 60.5 percent of the officers are Serbs (who comprise only 40.5 percent of the population, according to the latest census statistics), while another 8 percent of the officers are Montenegrins, "the purest Serbs" (who constitute a mere 2.5 percent of Yugoslavia's inhabitants). More than 65 percent of the generals are either Serb or Montenegrin.[15] These figures, reflecting still the ethnic composition of the old Partisan elite, indicate the possibility of mass desertion or disinclination to fight, in the event of war, on the part of members of disgruntled nationalities in the general ranks (as occurred, indeed, during the invasion of Yugoslavia in April 1941).

Moreover, the loyalty to Yugoslavia's central leadership of the Territorial Defense Forces, which are closely linked to the individual socialist republics, may be suspect. In this context, it is significant that Tito has mentioned the army being used "to defend the achievements of our revolution, if needed, from internal enemies," but has not made a comparable statement regarding the Territorial Defense units.[16] It is quite possible that Tito is disinclined to trust these local forces, during times of stress, not to join dissidents of the same nationality, rather than firing upon them.

The capability of the Yugoslav army to resist effectively a Warsaw Pact invasion without external assistance must be considered to be in question. Even a cursory glance at a topographical map of Yugoslavia reveals inherent weaknesses in the Yugoslav defense capacity.[17] The Warsaw Pact's southern group of forces in Hungary has on permanent station two full-strength Soviet tank divisions and two motor rifle divisions. These forces could be increased several times over within days by units drawn from the remaining 27 full-strength Soviet divisions (including 14 tank divisions) in Central and Eastern Europe and from another 30 Soviet divisions or so (including about 10 tank divisions) from the nearby Odessa, Carpathian, and Kiev military districts of the USSR, as well as most of the 7 Soviet airborne divisions. Thus, without undue strain, the Soviet Union could concentrate some 30 divisions, including about 12 tank and 5 airborne divisions (with more than 8,000 tanks altogether), not counting the forces of Russia's Warsaw Pact allies. These divisions would be deployed mainly in Hungary, facing the exposed plains of Slavonia and the Vojvodina. (These lowlands, an extension of the plains of Southern Hungary, stretch southward, just beyond the Sava and Danube rivers, into the northernmost portions of Bosnia and Serbia, and westward almost to the Adriatic coast of Croatia.)

The Soviet army probably would drive one spearhead into Slavonia, where there may be elements favorable to Soviet intervention among Croats, who have been embroiled for decades in strife with the local Serb minority.[18] Another spearhead might thrust into the Vojvodina, preferably accompanied at least by token units from the six divisions of the Hungarian army, who might be greeted as liberators by some segments of the Magyar population. The heavily outnumbered Yugoslav army, after full mobilization, would be able, optimally, to deploy the equivalent of some 15 to 18 divisions, many of them initially strung out along the Hungarian, Bulgarian, and, to a lesser degree, Albanian frontier areas. Not being equipped with adequate Precision Guided Munitions against tanks and aircraft, at least to date, the Yugoslav forces probably would find it impossible to prevent the Soviet armored "fists" from breaking through and rolling into the northern edges of Serbia proper and of Bosnia. The Territorial Defense Forces could have only very limited utility against Soviet armored columns, even if they could be regarded as completely reliable. Thus, Yugoslav forces almost certainly would have to retreat into the mountains of Serbia, Bosnia-Hercegovina, and Montenegro, where they might attempt to emulate the episode of relatively successful Partisan warfare waged by Tito's comrades and followers more than thirty years ago.

In fact, there have been reports in the Western press that Yugoslavia, attempting apparently to enhance its capability to resist Soviet armored threats, has requested from the United States the shipment of Precision Guided Anti-tank Munitions of the TOW category, sophisticated communications and radar equipment, and the F-16, which Yugoslavia wished to coproduce with the U.S. According to one source, American policy (or, to be more precise, the policy preference of former Secretary of State Kissinger) has been not to ship such systems to Yugoslavia until that state begins to support U.S. positions on important issues, most notably the Middle East and Puerto Rican independence. Another, perhaps more credible explanation of American reluctance to ship the TOW to Yugoslavia is that the United States fears that, should it sell such sophisticated main-line NATO weaponry to Yugoslavia, the Belgrade security apparatus might not prove sufficiently tight to guarantee that the systems in question did not end up in Moscow.[19]

In fact, late in 1976 reports were released to the Western press that the U.S. Secretary of Commerce (then Elliot Richardson) had obtained evidence concerning Yugoslav reexport to Russia of sophisticated American technology barred by the U.S. government from sale to the USSR, including computers, computerized components, and even entire computerized systems. Such action contravened the original U.S. stipulations of transfer of these items to Yugoslavia. The initial

American reaction to these discoveries was to cut off shipments of such systems until Yugoslavia had tightened its safeguards to prevent recurrence. Once Washington was convinced that Belgrade in fact had improved its security measures (or, perhaps more to the point, had committed itself to refrain from these practices), the U.S. did reinstate shipments on a case-by-case basis. A major problem remaining is that, as Soviet-Yugoslav commercial relations have expanded, more and more corporations in Yugoslavia have developed ties to the Soviet Union. Thus, even if the United States were convinced that the central government in Belgrade was not betraying American technological secrets, it could not be confident that individual members of corporations were not doing so as a result of "interpenetration" with their Soviet counterparts (although Washington has barred quite a number of such Yugoslav corporations from American technology sales).[20] This development has obvious implications for future transfer of sensitive U.S. technology, especially military technology, to Yugoslavia. The U.S. would have particular cause for anxiety if Yugoslavia were to be embroiled in armed conflict or were to suffer internal disintegration. Since Belgrade (assuming, once again, that it has not allowed the USSR to receive sensitive materiel as part of a deliberate policy of appeasing Moscow) apparently has encountered difficulties in controlling such transfers even during tranquil periods, the Yugoslav leaders presumably could exercise even less control in periods of turmoil and chaos. On the other hand, a decision to "starve" Yugoslavia with regard to materiel essential to the modernization of its armed forces might constitute a positive inducement for Moscow to intervene militarily in a post-Tito succession crisis.

In such an eventuality, the Warsaw Pact forces probably could drive straight through the low Croatian hills westward to the Adriatic, where they could subsequently move down the coast at a more leisurely pace in an effort to encircle the retreating Yugoslav army. If, simultaneously, the Bulgarian army, with supporting Soviet divisions, launched an attack into mountainous Macedonia, aided by landings of Soviet airborne units, elements of the local population (as in the Vojvodina) might welcome the invaders, given the Bulgar-Macedonian ethnic affinity, and the Territorial Defense Forces might refuse to fight. Divisions of the Soviet-Bulgarian command then could move northward from Macedonia to link up with units of the Soviet-Hungarian front in northeastern Serbia, thereby completing the encirclement of the Yugoslav army in its Bosnian-Montenegrin-Serbian mountain redoubt. It might not even prove necessary to pursue the Yugoslav forces into that encircled region. Belgrade itself, an exposed city, would long since have been captured, and the presumably demoralized surrounded forces of the Yugoslav army probably would have difficulty continuing the struggle—particularly as the desertion factor well might come into play at that juncture.

This entire scenario is reminiscent of the events of April 1941, when the Yugoslav state collapsed under pressure from Italians attacking (in the name of Albania) from the south, Italians invading from Italy in the west, Bulgarians and German forces moving in from the east, and German and Hungarian units attacking from the north. At that time, in part also because of collaboration with the invaders and desertion of Croat units, the northern plains fell to the enemy almost immediately. Bosnia, Montenegro, and Central Serbia, on the other hand, held out much better, owing to geography and the greater resolve of the local population (Partisans and Chetniks) to resist foreign occupation.

The Soviet perception concerning the manner in which Soviet and other Warsaw Pact units might be received by the local population could prove to be a crucial factor. Of course, even if the Territorial Defense Forces and various unhappy nationalities within the army were to remain loyal to Yugoslavia, as it is now constituted, the Soviet forces still would achieve eventual military victory. However, the Kremlin certainly would not want to reenact the debacle of the 1939-40 invasion of Finland, when the Red Army was held off for an embarrassingly long four months by a tiny Finnish defense force. Even the developments of 1956 and 1968, when Warsaw Pact "liberating" forces were met with enormous open hostility by the inhabitants of the invaded socialist states, would prove very embarrassing to Moscow if repeated in Yugoslavia. Either of these contingencies would have a demoralizing effect upon Soviet military personnel. (After Hungary, whole Soviet units had to be taken out of the lines for protracted "reorientation.") Most important of all, fighting in Yugoslavia, *if protracted long enough,* would make it increasingly difficult for NATO to sit by passively and watch the geostrategic situation in Southern Europe being changed decisively to its disadvantage. Thus, Soviet estimates of Yugoslav determination and cohesion are likely to prove a key to Moscow's decision on how to react to a Yugoslav succession crisis.

Precisely with this consideration in mind, Belgrade has begun to publicize, in unusually frank military detail, strategic reports like the following article in *Borba*:

An attempt by an aggressor, or group of aggressors, to invade Yugoslavia would be met by considerably stronger resistance than experienced by the aggressor in World War II. First of all, the Yugoslav Armed Forces are trained to fight in up-to-date combat conditions, and their training is based on experience gained in these conditions. The equipment of the Yugoslav Armed Forces equals, or even rivals, that of the most modern armed forces of Europe and the world. They are equipped with the most up-to-date anti-tank weapons—from hand-held grenade and rocket launchers to guided missiles, laser sights and other equipment for missile launching from helicopters and aircraft—capable of repelling a coordinated attack mounted by a force of several thousands of the most up-to-date tanks of any type. Precision-guided projectiles, which as a rule hit a mobile target with the first firing, have become a reality that any potential aggressor against Yugoslavia should take into account.

The capability for defending Yugoslav air space is no less impressive. The Yugoslav Armed Forces are equipped with the most up-to-date air defense system, which is capable of inflicting considerable damage on any potential aggressor. The greatest proportion of that equipment is already being manufactured in Yugoslavia, or is about to be in the near future. As far as the organization of supplies and equipment is concerned, all checks on Yugoslav readiness point to the fact that the Yugoslav Armed Forces are prepared to carry out successfully prolonged and most complex combat actions in modern conditions, which also imply a nuclear war.

The organization of Yugoslav defense, which is based on the participation of virtually the entire population within the framework of all-people's defense, means not only a great increase in Yugoslav forces by comparison with the enemy's but also represents a new type of combat action to which no aggressor can find an appropriate answer. This new concept of combat action is also justified by the fact that the number of civilians killed in modern warfare tends to exceed the number of casualties suffered by operational units. If this is the case, then why not [arm the] civilian population which will not only strengthen the resistance capability of a country but also, by being trained and equipped, reduce the number of casualties among its own ranks?

A clause in the Yugoslav constitution stipulating that no one can agree to capitulation robs the potential aggressor of the misuse of international law concerning the use of mass terror. Mass terror by the aggressor can also be ruled out by the ability of the entire people to wage war. However, should the use of mass terror be contemplated, or should nuclear or other weapons for mass destruction be used, our country may, in the framework of the general defense concept, reconsider its attitude toward the question of non-proliferation of nuclear weapons. Because today the possibility exists—both in the East and in the West—of manufacturing nuclear weapons costing a few hundred dollars instead of a few hundred million dollars as in the past. Cheap and easy manufacture of "mini-nuclear" weapons, capable of destroying entire units or headquarters of the aggressor, would have a sobering effect on anyone contemplating invasion of our country, and it is no exaggeration to state that mass terror comparable to that practised during the last war cannot ever again be carried out on the territory of Yugoslavia.

If the unity of the people, its readiness to resist any agressor and to defend the achievements of the thirty years of development are added to all this, it is possible to look into the future of Yugoslavia with confidence and equanimity.[21]

Tito's desire for weapons systems like TOW leaves observers to wonder just how accurate are *Borba*'s boasts regarding Yugoslav equipment in the field of Precision Guided Munition. (At the moment, the latter seems to consist primarily of

Soviet-manufactured items, such as the Sagger ATGW and the ZSU-57-2 SP AAA—probably with accompanying "Gun Dish" and "Fire Can" radars. The descriptions in *Borba*, however, suggest the acquisition of more sophisticated systems.)[22] With regard to *Borba*'s hints concerning Yugoslav nuclear weapons, it is generally believed that Belgrade still is some years away from developing a nuclear device, not to speak of deploying an adequate delivery system or attaining a sophisticated level of competence in the technologically complex field of miniaturization.

While such publications, therefore, clearly are intended to impress Moscow with Yugoslavia's determination to go to any lengths in resisting an invasion—and, as such, ought to be taken seriously by the Kremlin—the fact remains that any effective defense of the country will require massive military assistance from the West.

Should the NATO powers, during a crisis, wish to provide Yugoslavia with substantial shipments of arms and other materiel, the speediest and most direct supply route for such an operation would extend from major Western supply dumps in the German Federal Republic across Austrian territory to airports in Yugoslavia.[23] Such overflight would involve a clear violation of Austria's obligations as a neutral power under the 1955 State Treaty for the Re-establishment of an Independent and Democratic Austria.[24] However, the West would have difficulty finding convenient alternatives to overflight of Austria. A route extending south over Switzerland and then east over Italy would be far longer, its utilization would involve an Italian government which might have problems authorizing such an action (because of increasing participation of Communists in the governance of Italy), and, of course, would require permission of a Swiss state with a tradition of neutralism stronger (and older) than that of present-day Austria. Thus, supplies to Yugoslavia might have to be flown still further west, over France—assuming, as is by no means certain, that French permission were forthcoming—before swinging back east. These alternate routes would be very costly and inconvenient, as well as presenting diplomatic obstacles hardly less severe than those posed by Austria.

Direct flight from the United States, utilizing the C-5A Galaxy, would require either refueling at an air base (presumably the Azores) or midair refueling, since the full-capacity range of a C-5A is only about 3,700 miles (i.e., only some 70 percent of the full distance from the U.S. eastern seaboard to Yugoslavia).[25] Either of these contingencies would be costly, time-consuming, and restrictive in terms of the amount of materiel that could be transferred before Yugoslavia's military position was damaged irretrievably. Moreover, direct flight from America still would require the active cooperation of European states, either in allowing the Galaxies to land (remembering that, in the case of the Azores, the Portuguese government is less likely to be forthcoming than its predecessors), or in permitting refueling planes to take off from bases on their territory.

Sea-based resupply of Yugoslavia would be less practical still: In the first place, it would be prohibitively slow, even if originating at Hamburg, Bremen, or Portsmouth, rather than at U.S. ports. Moreover, it would require sending ships during wartime into the Adriatic—a narrow waterway that can be closed off, at least temporarily, by mines, not to speak of submarine or air attacks. Of course, mining the Straits of Otranto would constitute an escalatory action by the Warsaw Pact. However, if the USSR were willing to chance an invasion of Yugoslavia, time would be the crucial element in determining Western reactions: NATO would be confronted either with a fait accompli (an effective Soviet surgical operation with irreversible results—leaving no room for a Western military response) or, on the other hand, with a Soviet military incursion into a country that was resisting bitterly and slowing down the invaders (thus, in effect, leaving Western consciences with no alibi for nonintervention). This being the case, the Kremlin well might decide that it was worthwhile taking increased risk by mining the Straits of Otranto (an action that, in turn, would require minesweeping by the U.S. Sixth Fleet—a time-consuming operation), since it would provide the USSR with sufficient additional time to eliminate the main core of Yugoslav opposition.

For all of these reasons, overflight of Austria still might prove to be the most practical solution to the problem of resupplying Yugoslavia. The key question involved would be the potential reaction of the Austrian government.[26] While, in all probability, Vienna could not remain silent on the matter, the precise nature of its reaction might depend upon the circumstances in which the West felt compelled to resort to such a move. If the Austrians seemed prepared actually to shoot down cargo planes en route to Yugoslavia, the West well might pause before deciding to undertake such an operation. However, if Austria were willing merely to lodge a *pro forma* complaint—or even to take some token shots at transport planes, while taking great care not to hit any—the U.S. might be ready to risk public recrimination over a technical violation of international law. Objectively, the precedent of a nonaligned Yugoslavia being invaded hardly could prove palatable to the neutralist Austrians, and they might be expected to feel horrified at the prospect that such a state simply would be abandoned to its fate. However, relations between Austria and Yugoslavia have not been precisely amicable recently.

Despite—or, perhaps, rather because of—his own increased severity toward Slovenia, Tito has been pressuring Vienna with regard to the Slovene minority in Austria, located primarily in Carinthia, a province against which Tito advanced irredentist claims in 1945 and subsequently. He contends that Austria is

not living up to its obligations under the 1955 State Treaty—
specifically, Article 7, on the "Rights of the Slovene and Croat
Minorities" (see Appendix 4), and, to a lesser degree, Articles 6
(on Human Rights), 8 (on Democratic Institutions), and 9 (on
the Dissolution of Nazi Organizations). This last point relates
to clashes in Carinthia between Slovenes and members of the
right-wing German Heimatdienst association, as well as to the
alleged use of Austrian territory as a base for attacks upon
Yugoslav soil by members of the Ustasha.[27] Most of the
Yugoslav complaints revolve around charges of Germaniza-
tion of geographic place names in Carinthia and inadequate
educational and cultural facilities for the Slovene-speaking-
and-writing minority.[28] The implications for Austria of an
invocation of the 1955 State Treaty by Yugoslavia, a signatory
to the treaty, obviously are quite disturbing. Independent only
for some two decades, after undergoing Four-Power occupation, Austria is highly sensitive over questions of sovereignty.
Moreover, the Yugoslav press has been vituperative in its
condemnation of Austrian policy, accusing the Austrian federal and Klagenfurt municipal governments of being "negativist"
and "intolerant," while charging Chancellor Bruno Kreisky
with "moral and political cynicism of the first order."[29] Such
personal attacks hardly add warmth to the relationship between the Austrian and Yugoslav leaders; but, paradoxically,
neither can such dubious Yugoslav "compliments" as the
statement that it is easier to deal with an Austrian federal government headed by a "progressive man with socialist views"—a
comment sounding suspiciously like gratuitous interference in
Austrian domestic affairs that cannot but add grist to the mills
of the chancellor's political opponents.[30] Kreisky, on his part,
has attacked the Yugoslav (government-controlled) press,
terming it "intolerant, incendiary and generally unfree."[31]
Presumably he had in mind indiscriminate phrase-mongering
in Yugoslav newspapers, such as "ethnic slaughter."[32]

While there may be some basis for complaints by Carinthian Slovenes about their treatment, the entire issue appears to have been blown up out of all proportion. There has been periodic vandalism by German Carinthians—such as painting over the Slovenian version of place names on bilingual signposts, and by Slovene Carinthians—such as obliterating German language signposts.[33] In this connection, an Austrian census in 1976 was to determine whether the proportion of Slovenes in individual communities was sufficiently high (25 percent) to qualify for such ethnic benefits as bilingual signs. Slovenes, supported by Tito, claimed that the linguistic census would be exploited to limit their privileges, while the Austrian federal government asserted that it would be used to benefit the Slovene community.[34] The Slovenes threatened to boycott the census, or to register as Hebrew- or Chinese-speaking.[35] (This threat was implemented only in some cases.)

The Slovene complaints—at least to the degree that Tito has been willing to back them—are petty when compared to the sufferings of East European minorities which really *do* live under oppression (particularly in the USSR). Actually, Yugoslavs in Austria enjoy privileges denied to other minorities: for instance, the Slovenes receive well over .75 million schillings per annum from the federal government for cultural activities, and the Burgenland Croats, who appear reasonably content, receive almost .50 million schillings, while the quiescent Hungarian and Czech minorities receive no such allocations.[36]

Certainly such disparities as do exist would not appear to warrant the strong language used by Belgrade against the Austrian government and Chancellor Kreisky. In any case, such rhetoric—even were it justified—hardly would be calculated to render Austria more sympathetic to Yugoslavia's plight, should Vienna be asked to allow the West (at least tacitly) to overfly Austrian territory in order to save Belgrade. There does not appear to be any rational explanation just why Marshal Tito should have considered this a propitious time to irritate his Austrian neighbors.

9

A Belgrade-Moscow
Rapprochement?

There is some suspicion in the West that Tito perhaps has
been appeasing Moscow, in recent years, to such a degree that
he may be foreclosing the options of his successors. As mentioned previously, since 1974 the Soviet Union has been
obtaining increased port facilities along the Yugoslav Adriatic
coast. There have been repeated reports that Soviet officers, in
fairly significant numbers, have established a presence in major
Yugoslav ports. Moreover, Belgrade has granted the Soviet
Union overflight rights (so that the USSR might give logistical
support to its overseas clients) on at least two critical occasions
in recent times. According to one source, the Yugoslav government also has been permitting ongoing Soviet reconnaissance overflights en route to the Mediterranean—presumably
for "shadowing" and tracking purposes related to the movements of the U.S. Sixth Fleet.[1] Thus, Marshal Tito appears to
have been letting the Soviet Union obtain its military desiderata in the area, at least to a limited extent.

On the economic side, there is no question but that there has been considerable Yugoslav movement toward the Eastern bloc during this same period. To a significant degree this has been necessitated by the recession in Western Europe, which has caused the number of Yugoslav *Gastarbeiter* to decrease from 1,100,000 at the end of 1973 to some 900,000 at the end of 1975, with prospects for further decline. A portion of the returning workers has moved to Eastern Europe—particularly Czechoslovakia, where it seems that more than 10,000 Yugoslav temporary workers were employed in 1976.[2] Apparently a few hundred Yugoslav workers even have been dispatched to the Soviet Union.[3] The economic ties between the two states were among the major topics of discussion at the Brezhnev-Tito summit meeting of November 1976. Trade between the two countries amounted to some $6 billion for the period 1971-76, and is expected to reach $14 billion for the period 1976-80, according to the Belgrade journal *Politika*.[4] Since total Yugoslav foreign trade has averaged about $12 billion annually between 1974 and 1976, if that level were to continue, Soviet-Yugoslav trade would constitute around 20 to 25 percent of all Yugoslav foreign trade during the next five years. The trade shift toward Comecon is demonstrated graphically in the table on page 111. (It should be noted, however, that this trend did not continue into the first quarter of 1977, when Yugoslav exports to the USSR and Czechoslovakia declined by one-third, according to the Belgrade *Indeks* of April 1977.)

While Yugoslavia, of course, is not a member of Comecon, it does have observer status on several committees. Since, in the past, one of the reasons given by Yugoslavia for the absence of a more dynamic trade relationship was "the lack of an institutional framework," it may be logical to assume that as the volume of trade increases, so too will the institutional ties.[5] (In this connection, it is interesting to note that the Russian chairman of Comecon's Investment Bank visited Belgrade in

Regional Distribution of Yugoslavia's Foreign Trade
(in percentages)

Area	Exports				Imports			
	1973	1974	1975	1976 Jan-June	1973	1974	1975	1976 Jan-June
Developed Western countries	55.1	45.1	35.4	42.1	61.1	58.7	57.5	55.3
Comecon countries	32.3	38.6	46.8	43.3	24.4	22.7	24.2	29.1
Developing countries	12.6	16.3	17.8	14.6	14.4	18.6	18.3	15.6

Source: *Ekonomska politika*, April 26 and June 28, 1976, quoted in Zdenko Antic, "Yugoslavia on the Way to Economic Recovery," RFE RAD Background Report 229, Yugoslavia (November 9, 1976), p. 6.

June 1976.)[6] Regardless of whether these ties do increase, Soviet links with the Yugoslav economy probably will help to develop groups within Yugoslavia that have strong vested interests in close Yugoslav-Soviet relations, both political and economic (presumably, the latter to some degree are connected to the former). According to Soviet sources, by late 1975 more than two hundred firms and organizations in Yugoslavia had ties to Soviet trade organizations.[7] As mentioned previously, some of these Yugoslav firms have been suspected of transferring American technology illegally to the Soviet Union, whether with or without Tito's connivance.

The Soviet Union appears to be attempting to bring about greater integration of the East European and Soviet economies; this is borne out by the influx of workers from Communist countries into the more remote regions of the USSR[8] and by the Brezhnev statement to Ceauşescu regarding the need for "perfecting the socialist division of labor." Thus, increased ties between Yugoslavia and the Soviet Union may fit well into a comprehensive Soviet policy calling for economic absorption of the other Communist countries.

In addition to Yugoslav concessions to the Soviet Union in the military sphere and increased ties to the Russian economy, Belgrade appears also to have been moving toward the USSR politically and ideologically. While it is true that Tito agreed to show up at the East Berlin conference only after a considerable amount of negotiations and concessions on both sides, nevertheless it was significant that Yugoslav representatives were prepared to participate at all in a Communist conference sponsored by East Germany—which, traditionally, along with Bulgaria, has been a symbol of supine subservience to Moscow. The Kremlin has sought Yugoslavia's participation at such a conference for some time, since, in view of ideological bickering between the two Communist parties, the very presence of the Yugoslavs symbolizes that the international Communist movement remains cohesive enough to assemble under the aegis of Moscow (or of its East German surrogate). Moreover, the conference document, to which the participating parties assented, was sufficiently ambiguous for the USSR to interpret it, at least publicly, as embracing the Soviet position—particularly the reference to "internationalist . . . solidarity." (Moscow chose to ignore the qualification "voluntary," included at the behest of the more "revisionist" European Communist parties.)[9]

"Internationalist solidarity" and "socialist internationalism" have become code phrases for the Brezhnev Doctrine; thus, concessions on this issue, however qualified, have dangerous implications. This became evident rapidly when Brezhnev, during his consolidation of power which culminated in the ouster of his rival N. Podgorny, promulgated a new Soviet constitution in 1977. Article 30 of the new draft immediately set the alarm bells ringing in Belgrade, since it stated:

As a component part of the socialist system, of the socialist community, the Soviet Union shall promote and strengthen friendship, cooperation and comradely mutual assistance with the socialist countries on the basis of socialist internationalism, and shall actively participate in economic integration and in international socialist division of labor.[10]

The authoritative Belgrade daily *Politika* expressed dismay at the implications for Yugoslavia and other dissident Communist countries of this elevation of the Brezhnev Doctrine to constitutional status. *Politika* was concerned no less at the campaign to synchronize the constitutions of the East European satellite regimes with the new Soviet draft. If these countries were to adopt constitutions modeled on the Soviet document, as suggested by the Czechoslovak Communist Party daily *Rude Pravo,* Russian intervention in Eastern Europe would be sanctioned a priori by the legitimization in Article 30 of "socialist internationalism."[11] Moreover, the reference to "international socialist division of labor" augurs badly for the type of economic autonomy defended by the Romanians, since it is a code phrase for compulsory integration of East European economies under Soviet control.

In terms of domestic politics, Tito has moved away considerably from the "liberal" brand of communism which emerged in Yugoslavia after the 1948 expulsion from the Cominform. During recent years Tito's repression of individual liberties and of ethnic minorities has begun to resemble somewhat the domestic situation in the Soviet Union (even if the Yugoslav brand of "socialism" differs from the Soviet version in the economic realm). Belgrade itself conceded in the late summer of 1976 that it had broken up thirteen "illegal opposition" groups and arrested 237 of their members. (Outside sources claim that many more persons have been arrested, and certainly many emigrés have been "dealt with" in one form or another by the UDBA.)[12] Thus, if the "Cominformists" or any other group were to impose a Soviet-style regime upon Yugoslavia, the contrast might not be so very startling. Indeed, recently Belgrade has opened a press campaign against Western support for human rights and for East European dissidents.[13] Moreover, during the Belgrade preparatory meeting for the follow-up conference to the 1975 Helsinki accords, the Yugoslav authorities took drastic measures, including expulsion of Western participants attempting to express solidarity with Soviet Jewish dissidents.

If the concessions to the Soviet Union made by Tito really are as far-reaching potentially as implied by some of the data presented here, this is very difficult to explain rationally from Belgrade's vantage point. However, according to one source, part of Tito's rationale stems from a confidential warning received from Brezhnev; the Soviet Communist Party leader reportedly claimed that, while he himself had no aggressive designs upon Yugoslavia, there were certain unnamed "hard-liners" in the Kremlin who did. Thus, if the Kremlin were unable to point to tangible gains in relations with Belgrade, Brezhnev is said to have alleged, these "hard-liners" would gain ascendancy and Yugoslavia would be greatly endangered.[14] In fact, this gambit is quite hoary and has been used by the Soviet Union in past dealings with Tito. Most notable was an incident during the spring of 1961, when the Soviet Union violated a moratorium on atmospheric nuclear weapons tests reached with the United States, at the very time when the conference of "nonaligned" states was meeting in Belgrade. Apparently the "nonaligned" conference was on the verge of condemning the USSR for this breach when Tito received an urgent message from Khrushchev stating that the Soviet leader had committed himself in Moscow to a pro-Tito policy and that, if a conference convened by Tito denounced the USSR, certain "hard-liners" would gain ascendancy in the Kremlin and turn against the Yugoslav regime. Tito apparently "bought" Khrushchev's argument, and the nonaligned conference abandoned its intention to condemn the USSR. Brezhnev's November 1976 assertion that the scenario of a Yugoslav "Little Red Riding Hood" confronted by a Soviet "terrible and bloodthirsty wolf" was a mere fairy tale may have been intended as an earnest of his own allegedly innocuous intentions. In any event, the "moderate" Brezhnev (the very man who authored the Brezhnev Doctrine) thus, without firing a shot in anger, may have garnered some of the very same Yugoslav concessions that a "hard-line" Brezhnev might have hoped to achieve.

One explanation for the apparent cooling of relations between Bucharest and Belgrade has been that Ceauşescu feels let down by the concessions Tito has made to the USSR, not least in the context of the East Berlin meeting.[15] This thesis would appear to be substantiated by Romanian statements made after the conference, expressing appreciation of the strongly autonomist positions taken by the Italian, French, and Spanish Communist parties, but failing to mention the Yugoslav party.[16] If this version is correct, it might explain why Ceauşescu himself has started to appease Moscow—he feels isolated and vulnerable now that Tito has "sold out" (as Bucharest would view it).[17]

There are rumors in Belgrade to the effect that Tito has asked Brezhnev for some kind of "guarantee" that Yugoslavia will not be invaded during the succession period; it seems difficult to believe that a hard-bitten Communist veteran could be so naive. However, this might explain some of Tito's less comprehensible actions during the last couple of years. Of course, by going so far in the direction of meeting Moscow's desiderata in the military, economic, and political fields, the Yugoslav leader not only may be diminishing the Kremlin's incentive to resort to armed force against the post-Tito regime;

he also may be depriving his successors of any meaningful autonomy vis-à-vis the USSR or, at least, undermining their ability to resist Soviet pressure, not to speak of a Russian invasion.

Tito himself appears to have become aware recently that the widespread impression that he is inclined to appease Moscow may have a deleterious impact on Bucharest, on the mood of the Yugoslav people, and, not least, on the West. Consequently, Yugoslav representatives have "leaked" detailed information concerning the alleged military aspects of the Tito-Brezhnev meeting in November 1976. According to these reports, Brezhnev presented forty proposals of a military nature, including *permanent* overflight rights across Yugoslavia for Soviet military and civilian aircraft, the transformation of the port of Kotor into a permanent Soviet naval base (rather than a facility for supply and repairs, as heretofore), and the assignment of a high-ranking Yugoslav officer to the Military Council of the Warsaw Pact in Moscow. Tito is said to have rejected flatly these Soviet requests. The "leaks" were reported after a seven-week period during which Tito's representatives refused to discuss these aspects of the November meeting.[18]

The dangers inherent in Tito's vacillations vis-à-vis Moscow appear to have caused alarm in some Belgrade circles, particularly among officers of the Yugoslav army. Colonel-General Ivan Kukoc, a member of the Executive Committee of the Presidium of the Central Committee of the Yugoslav League of Communists, recently voiced implicit criticism of Tito's policy of placing major reliance upon the Soviet Union as a source of Yugoslavia's weapons systems. He drew the following analogy (apparently with Israel's position of dependency on American arms during the 1973 Yom Kippur War, which prevented Israel from annihilating the encircled Egyptian Third Army—a rather daring reference in view of Tito's personal commitment to a pro-Arab policy):

> Factually, contemporary wars, just as the latest wars in the Middle East, have shown that the success of a country which does not have basic sources of its armament, and even success in a war which it is conducting, is conditioned by the behavior of the country on which it relies for its armaments.[19]

10
Scenarios and Policy Options

From the analyses presented in this study, several scenarios emerge, with the common denominator of a massive Soviet thrust to monopolize influence in Yugoslavia after Tito. (No consideration has been given here to developments of smaller concern to the West, since they appear less probable and because it is evident that they do not require urgent preventive planning on the part of the United States.) A "worst contingency" approach cannot be avoided, if a study of this kind is to be useful.

The contingency that naturally draws most attention is the specter of a replay of the April 1941 drama, this time in the form of overt Soviet military intervention on the pretext of "liberating" minority nationalities from the "yoke" of (Serb-dominated) Yugoslav centralism. The ethnic groups that may contain significant elements prepared to cooperate with foreign powers, including even the USSR, in the hope of attaining genuine self-government (and, perhaps, full independence) probably include the Croats, the Macedonians, and possibly the Albanians. In the case of the Croats, emigrés and *Gastar-*

beiter pose greater problems than those who stayed home, while the reaction of the Albanians will be influenced by Tirana's posture. It is significant that the manifesto published by the Croat terrorists who hijacked a Trans World Airlines jet in September 1976, calling themselves the "Croatian National Liberation Forces," made specific reference to the claims of other ethnic groups:

> Besides the fact that, inside Yugoslavia, a sustained genocidal politic [sic] is being perpetrated upon the Croatian nation, the Albanian nation is likewise biologically threatened. Belgrade holds, under its occupation, a large portion of Albanian national territory, on which virtually half of the Albanian population is settled. The Belgrade occupation forces also command a part of Bulgarian and Hungarian national territory.

This clear signal that at least one Croat separatist group is willing to cooperate with other separatists and even with foreign irredentist forces does not augur well for Tito's successors. Of course, whether the Macedonians, Albanians, and Hungarians in Yugoslavia really wish to be reunited with kinsmen in neighboring states is another question. Nevertheless, the potential for cooperation between groups from various discontented nationalities would appear to exist.[1] It is even conceivable, given the increased alienation of Moslems and Slovenes in the last few years, that Bosnia and Slovenia may present a significant problem to Belgrade, despite the relative tranquility of these republics during most of Tito's reign.

This study has dealt extensively with the secessionist scenarios because of several considerations.

Fairly widespread contacts appear to have been established between the USSR and members of dissident ethnic minority groups, both in Yugoslavia and among emigrés. Propagandistically, this might provide a viable option for the Kremlin—at least vis-à-vis supporters of the non-Muscovite left (Communist and non-Communist); the USSR could adopt the posture of intervening on behalf of the (once again fashionable) principle of national self-determination (viz., the Basques, Catalans, Corsicans, Scots, Québécois, etc.). Thus, the Soviet Union might be able to engineer such overt intervention without having to pay too high a price in terms of public opinion.

Countries of the "Third World"—particularly those purporting to belong to the "nonaligned" camp, in which Tito long has attempted to play a leading role—probably would react with mixed feelings: On the one hand, for some time they have made a fetish of the legitimacy of resort to armed force, even by elements that are nonindigenous or operate from foreign bases, in support of "national liberation" (e.g., Angola, Rhodesia, Laos, Cambodia, Bangladesh, Algeria). On the other hand, in most cases they themselves are highly vulnerable to ethnic separatism (e.g., the problems posed by the Ibos in Nigeria, the Kurds in Iraq, the Pathans in Pakistan). These two conflicting sentiments may be expected to neutralize one another, reducing the global "costs" of Soviet military action to "aid" dissident nationalities, and leaving one to wonder why Tito has invested so much in his Third World relationships, frequently at the expense of his vital links with the West.

On the "benefits" side of the ledger, the USSR could make a distinct impact on the global balance, not only because of the very tangible tactical and strategic implications of a successful invasion of Yugoslavia (discussed in Chapter 7), but also because of the psychological effects on world perceptions of such an exhibition of Soviet "determination" and of Western "flagging will." Consequently, this is an issue of major significance in the struggle for global hegemony, requiring early and intensive consideration on the part of U.S. and NATO decision makers.

From a purely diplomatic/juridical point of view, the array of response options available to Washington is not devoid of rays of light. To mention only one aspect, the United States and its allies could extend military assistance to Belgrade (in materiel and, conceivably, even manpower) as a legitimate act in defense of a universally recognized state against unprovoked aggression. Such actions would be in full harmony with the basic premises of the (Western) international system. This apparently formalistic point is not without political significance: The mobilization (in America and among its European allies) of public support for an appropriate response would become incomparably easier, particularly since Yugoslavia, unlike Hungary and Czechoslovakia, could not be written off as "belonging" to the Soviet "sphere." Without resolving, at this point, the question of whether full-scale (or more limited) counterintervention *would* or *could* constitute the appropriate response, there should be no illusions, at any rate, that the issue can be evaded by a Western decision to "refuse to pick up the gauntlet," i.e., to ignore Soviet actions in Yugoslavia. The rest of the world hardly ever did (nor does it seem to now) regard a refusal to respond to an adversary's challenge as a deliberate "self-denying ordinance," rather than as a sign of weakness. In other words, a "refusal to pick up the gauntlet" is viewed precisely as would be an unsuccessful attempt to withstand an adversary, namely as a defeat—with all the global repercussions of being regarded as the losing party.

There remains the question of whether the United States could respond to overt Soviet moves by covert actions, and what preemptive or anticipatory steps the West might take now to deter Soviet intervention plans. The former possibility appears to be circumscribed sharply by increasing American domestic constraints on almost all covert operations, other than pure intelligence gathering, and by time and scale factors: Covert actions necessarily are time-consuming, and, by definition, their visibility (and thus their magnitude) is limited— while Soviet overt intervention, for reasons analyzed earlier, would have to be as massive and swift as possible.

Moreover, in this context, as well as in connection with the adoption of a timely and credible Western deterrent posture (discussed below), the cooperation or, at least, collusion of Marshal Tito would be most helpful. The old Partisan leader, however, seems to have convinced himself in recent years that the Kremlin can be "bought off" (or the inevitable at least postponed) by appeasement and the pretense in public that he is convinced of Moscow's good faith. In less official ways, however, Tito has managed to convey to the outside world his anxieties about Soviet pressure, particularly concerning military concessions, as well as his willingness, under certain circumstances, to stand up to the Kremlin—provided the requisite degree of Western backing were forthcoming. (Reports "leaked" by Belgrade concerning the military requests Brezhnev supposedly placed before Tito at their meeting in November of 1976 were interpreted in NATO circles as a broad hint that the West should prepare for the contingency of possible Soviet action against Yugoslavia during the succession period.)

Of course, variations on the basic theme of Soviet intervention in support of centrifugal forces would include also various scenarios of Soviet *covert* or surrogate assistance to groups seeking national autonomy or independence. If successful, such Russian aid would leave these separatist elements beholden to and, in effect, dependent on Moscow. This approach would be virtually free of costs in terms of any international embarrassment to the USSR, and it might prove very difficult for an American president to react to such Soviet moves, particularly considering adverse congressional reaction to

United States covert aid to Angolan groups in 1975-76. However, it is questionable whether Soviet covert aid would suffice to change the status quo, i.e., whether indigenous centrifugal elements in Yugoslavia could attain the strength to prevail with outside assistance short of full-scale Soviet military intervention. Nor is it clear whether Moscow necessarily would opt for dismemberment of the state that Tito built, if reasonably promising alternatives became apparent.

In this context, a second basic scenario would lead to the emergence of a strongly "centralist" Serb-Montenegrin regime (essentially military, in all probability), which would lean heavily on the supporting arm of the Kremlin in order to "discourage" the dissolution of the multiethnic state at the hands of various separatist movements. It would be most difficult for the United States to respond effectively to such a Soviet policy, since a Western government—even if acting on behalf of what may be perceived widely as legitimate aspirations for national self-determination—hardly could intervene to oppose a recognized government in Eastern Europe, particularly after assenting to the Helsinki accords. From this viewpoint, the more clearly and quickly and new "centralist" federal leadership in Belgrade were ensconced in power, the harder it would become for Washington to operate against it— irrespective of the degree of its dependency on Moscow, and regardless of how tenuous its control might be in the non-Serb portions of Yugoslavia. Thus, this second basic scenario, if it were to unfold, would prove quite advantageous to the Soviet Union. However, a unified "centralist" Belgrade leadership might not need or request Soviet aid in constraining or subduing restive anti-Serb elements, particularly if the situation were not desperate. Indeed, if the USSR and its Bulgarian or Hungarian allies were not involved in inciting, encouraging, and aiding dissident ethnic groups, the situation probably would not deteriorate to a crisis point, especially since the loyalty and support of the Yugoslav armed forces for Belgrade would seem assured against separatists (given the predominance of Serb-Montenegrin elements in the officer corps).

A third scenario is based upon a Yugoslav succession crisis caused mainly by factional, rather than primarily ethnic strife, with Moscow (particularly the Soviet security agencies) assisting one of the competing groups and bringing to power a regime beholden to the USSR. A factional struggle, waged essentially within the confines of Belgrade and not involving overt or large-scale resort to armed force, would be difficult for the West to influence, short of actually dispatching manpower at the request of one party. Covert Western aid hardly could compete with KGB and GRU elements that cannot but have become intertwined with significant segments of the Yugoslav elite (as a result of intimate arrangements, both in the military and economic sectors, that have been discussed previously). Moreover, the Kremlin could resort to tactically timed pronouncements for the purpose of strengthening the position of a preferred faction. Thus, for example, if Belgrade "Cominformists" wished to stress the need for closer alignment with Moscow because of the necessity of appeasing the USSR—the preponderant power in the Southeastern Europe/Eastern Mediterranean region—the Soviet Union could reinforce this line with truculent public statements and/or military maneuvers or other conspicuous demonstrations of Soviet military might and determination. If, on the other hand, a pro-Moscow faction wished to take an alternate approach and stress the positive gains to be made from links with the USSR, Moscow could respond accordingly, for example with offers of economic assistance.

The West, too, might attempt to influence developments in Yugoslavia during such a period through some form of signalling. However, the United States and its allies are likely to be laboring under a disadvantage in this respect: Western credibility cannot be presumed to be very high with regard to any show of force in Southeastern Europe—partly as a consequence of America's perceived failures of will (for instance in Southeast Asia and Angola) and partly because of some rather unfortunate pronouncements, concerning Yugoslavia, by Mr. Carter (during the presidential campaign), and, concerning the region as a whole, by President Ford and Mr. Helmut Sonnenfeldt. (The impact of these statements is discussed below.) Moreover, it is doubtful whether the United States has done much to build up organized cadres of likely allies within Yugoslavia, comparable to the "Cominformists" in potential access to the centers of power. Thus, the USSR may have distinct advantages in coordinating operations with Yugoslav factions that are under its wing.

A fourth scenario, which essentially is a variation of the third, would find a pro-Moscow faction in Belgrade emerging victoriously, more or less spontaneously, as a result of the significant concessions that Tito appears to have made to the Soviet Union, roughly during the period from 1974 onward. (These include his grant of port facilities on the Adriatic coast to Soviet naval units, his consent to the prolonged presence of Soviet officers in Dalmatian port areas, his decision to make an appearance at the East Berlin conference of Communist parties, his sniping at the human rights campaign, and his highly publicized, warm greetings extended to Brezhnev when the latter came to Belgrade in the fall of 1976—reportedly to arrange for further integration of the Yugoslav economy into the Comecon network.) If Tito indeed has laid the groundwork for Yugoslavia to slide back, to some extent, under Soviet tutelage (by sins of commission as well as omission), then obviously there would be little that Washington could do to prevent this process from gathering its own momentum. (The future alone will tell whether recent Yugoslav "leaks," to the effect that Tito decided to reject Brezhnev's more exorbitant military requests in November 1976, and even more recent indications that the growth in Yugoslav-Soviet trade may have been halted, signify that the Yugoslav leader finally has developed doubts about the utility of appeasing Moscow.)

In the case of several of the earlier scenarios, a major factor affecting Soviet policy decisions concerning post-Tito Yugoslavia is likely to be Western adroitness in "signalling" and in the credible orchestration thereof. This could be of particular significance if the possibility of overt intervention were being considered by the USSR. As was explained earlier, Washington would be left with relatively credible response options in the case of the first scenario discussed—i.e., overt Soviet military assistance to separatist groups in Yugoslavia; however, this is not the only contingency in which the United States might attempt to influence Soviet behavior with respect to developments in Yugoslavia.

Regrettably, 1975 and 1976 witnessed almost classic examples of nullifying rather than maximizing American influence and ability to inculcate the seeds of restraint among Kremlin policy-makers. Specifically, these were the so-called "Sonnenfeldt Doctrine" and the comments made concerning Yugoslavia by the (then) presidential candidate, Mr. Carter, in a public appearance late in the 1976 presidential campaign—which were given subsequent reinforcement during the third presidential campaign debate between Mr. Carter and Mr. Ford. Cumulatively, these statements could easily be interpreted by Soviet leaders as a carte blanche, in effect, for the USSR to "deal with" Yugoslavia as "real estate" within the Soviet sphere of influence. While the United States understandably would not wish to limit its options in advance by committing itself publicly to the defense of Yugoslavia as that state is constituted at present, neither would it be in America's interests to indicate that Moscow should feel perfectly at ease in resorting to Soviet military might in Southeastern Europe. Rather, a sensible policy would seem to require subtle American intimation to the USSR that Washington just might take sufficient exception to high-level forcible Soviet intervention in the affairs of Yugoslavia to merit some tangible Western response, either in the region in question or, perhaps, elsewhere on the globe.[2] Warnings prior to such a crisis need not necessarily be public or even explicit. Deliberately ambiguous statements keeping open American response options might be sufficient to lend some degree of credence even to implicit American admonitions, public or private, particularly if supplemented by appropriate actions—perhaps including military maneuvers. In other words, a posture of American "planned unpredictability" is required, of the type that existed until the early 1970s, creating an impression of inscrutability that would make it inadvisable for Moscow to take American inaction for granted.

Unfortunately, the pronouncements made at a meeting of American ambassadors in London during December 1975 by State Department Counselor Helmut Sonnenfeldt, far from orchestrating the required degree of ambiguity in America's posture toward Eastern Europe, left little room for doubt in the Kremlin that America intended to respond feebly to a potential crisis in that part of the world. Regardless of its intent, or later emendations, the statement "It must be our policy to strive for an education that makes the relationship between the Eastern Europeans and the Soviet Union an organic one" certainly would appear to indicate that the United States considered Eastern Europe to be legitimately within the sphere of Soviet domination. Consequently, active American responses to Soviet actions within that region were less than likely. Sonnenfeldt's more specific reference to Yugoslavia, while indicating its importance to the West, hardly implied willingness on the part of Washington to *act* on behalf of Yugoslav independence. Included almost as a parenthetical afterthought, and apparently addressing itself more to Yugoslav than to Soviet behavior, this reference could do little to mitigate the initial effects of the main body of the statement. Sonnenfeldt asserted that "of course" State Department officials "accept that Yugoslav behavior will continue to be . . . influenced and constrained by Soviet power." It is noteworthy that he described any potential return of Yugoslavia to the Soviet orbit merely as a "major strategic setback" that warranted concern and worry on the part of the West, whereas the national Democratic platform of 1976 later described it as "a grave threat to peace."[3] Unquestionably, Belgrade was upset by his statement, and Tito made his feelings known to the West through an interview in the Greek newspaper *Kathimerini:*

> Instead of aspiring, in the spirit of Helsinki, to the integration of Europe as a whole, today stress is again being laid on strengthening bloc structures. Such a situation is no guarantee of European security. If this truth is not understood, a serious stagnation in European trends may take place.[4]

Moreover, the USSR apparently has taken due cognizance of the "Sonnenfeldt Doctrine," incorporating its language into Soviet public pronouncements. General Secretary Brezhnev's June 29, 1976, speech to the European Communist conference in East Berlin, for example, stressed the "profound organic and ever growing" ties between the Communist parties and states of Eastern Europe.[5] Thus, it seems that the Soviet Union considers the "doctrine" to be sufficiently representative of American policy to warrant its reiteration in official Soviet statements.

Mr. Carter's references to Yugoslavia, if anything, were less ambiguous and, thus, potentially even more damaging than the Sonnenfeldt statements. Unlike Sonnenfeldt's remarks which may not have been originally intended for general consumption, the Carter comments were presented in front of the world press and eventually repeated, in essence, before millions of television viewers during the third presidential campaign debate. During a press conference on October 16, 1976, he made the following statement:

> I would never go to war, become militarily involved in the internal affairs of another country, unless our own military security were directly threatened, and I don't believe that our security would be directly threatened if the Soviet Union went into Yugoslavia.[6]

This position, if promulgated as official U.S. policy, very likely would deprive putative Kremlin "moderates" of any ammunition against a proposed Soviet military intervention since they would no longer be able to warn their rivals with credibility about the dangers of a possible American response to such a Soviet operation. In fact, having declared Yugoslavia practically irrelevant to the security of this country, if Carter as president were now to reappraise his evaluation, he probably would encounter some difficulty in justifying to Congress and the American public the necessity of extending U.S. aid to friendly forces within Yugoslavia. The Carter statement, with some legitimacy, has been compared to the famous public pronouncement by Dean Acheson, then secretary of state, in which he failed to include South Korea within the American defense perimeter.[7]

With respect to these American statements regarding the future of Yugoslavia, it is relevant to bear in mind an additional factor. Unfortunately Tito's recent behavior, in terms both of increased repression within Yugoslavia and also of the (probably related) displays of Yugoslav truculence toward Western states and citizens, hardly places Belgrade in a favorable position to receive support from the West in a future crisis.

The Sonnenfeldt remark that "we would like [the Yugoslavs] to be less obnoxious, and we should allow them to get away with very little," no doubt referred to these phenomena.

Perhaps the most blatant example recently of Yugoslav abuse of a Western national was the case of Laszlo Toth, a naturalized American citizen who had emigrated from Yugoslavia and returned to his former homeland for a visit. Toth, a chemical engineer for a U.S. sugar company, took photographs of a Yugoslav sugar plant, reportedly with the permission of the manager of the factory, whereupon he was arrested by the local authorities and eventually sentenced to seven years' imprisonment for violations of Yugoslav security. It was only after the U.S. ambassador to Belgrade, Mr. Laurence Silberman—acting, apparently, against the wishes of State Department bureaucrats in Washington—proceeded to publicize the case to the point at which it became embarrassing to Tito that Toth finally was released, having served a year and a half in prison.[8] Similarly, Tito's truculence toward Austria in recent months, as well as increased repression of liberal, religious, and nationalist elements, the press, and the judiciary, hardly could be calculated to influence Western public opinion in favor of active support for Belgrade.

While Tito's recent policy has been repugnant indeed, and while the West should not desist from pursuing the type of energetic opposition to repression demonstrated by Mr. Silberman in the Toth case, nevertheless the United States cannot but recognize its vital interest in sustaining an independent Yugoslav state. Therefore, Washington ought to keep its options open, particularly in its public pronouncements. If a situation should arise which encouraged Soviet leaders to consider radical "solutions" to their long-standing Yugoslav "problem," they should have to bear in mind the *possibility* that America might not stand by idly while a key political and strategic position was being absorbed into the Soviet camp.

Conclusion

Perhaps more than anything else, this analysis seems to indicate that the intricately interwoven domestic and international factors shaping Yugoslavia's future render extremely tenuous any unqualified and dogmatic conclusions regarding that country's fate after Tito passes from the scene. However, as discussed at some length in this study, it does seem that considerable potential exists for developments in the succession period which would prove highly injurious to Western interests.

The Soviet Union, together with at least two of Yugoslavia's Warsaw Pact neighbors, Hungary and Bulgaria, collectively are endowed with the required military strength and the geographic location, as well as the political, territorial, and strategic incentives, to interfere in a Yugoslav state beset with internal difficulties during a post-Tito transition stage. These incentives might be counterbalanced, at least to some degree, by constraints, for instance in the form of Russian concern about the ramifications for Western Communist parties of blatant Soviet interference in the affairs of a sovereign Communist state. However, it is by no means established that, even if such a deleterious impact upon these Communist parties could be anticipated, it would, in fact, prove to be of a lasting nature. Nor, for that matter, is it clear that the Soviet leaders necessarily would be perturbed about such potential effects— at least not to a degree that would cause them to forego an opportunity for settling the "Yugoslav question" after three decades of intermittent difficulties with Belgrade.

Perhaps the only true deterrent to high-level Soviet and Warsaw Pact interference can come from the West. Signals of American determination (comparable to President Johnson's "Don't unleash the dogs of war" statement) or grave expressions of anticipatory concern (as contained in the 1976 national Democratic platform) could provide ammunition to putative "moderates" in a Politburo debate about the merits of various Soviet contingency plans for Yugoslavia. While Warsaw Pact military strength in the region well may be greater than that of NATO, the Soviet Union would have to consider possible American economic and political retaliation, or, perhaps, even American responses of a more military nature, directed toward other areas where the Soviet Union may be vulnerable.

Moreover, the United States would be capable of aiding Yugoslavia without necessarily committing American troops to the conflict. The dispatch of weapons systems or even initial electronic surveillance and intelligence aid could lengthen the duration of active Yugoslav resistance, thereby increasing the costs of invasion to the Soviet Union in terms of the danger of a tangible Western reponse, of Soviet casualties, and presumably also of international embarrassment. The USSR surely would not be pleased at the prospect of another protracted conflict along the lines of the 1940 Soviet-Finnish War. Thus, a determined American leadership, prepared to orchestrate in credible fashion a series of signals to Moscow that Western inaction should not be taken for granted if Russia intervened in

Yugoslavia, might deter the Kremlin from launching a cata-strophic "Operation Sarajevo."

By any standards, the fate of Tito's state is likely to prove of the greatest significance to the outcome of the East-West struggle for global "hegemony." Regrettably, Tito's own actions recently, in making significant concessions to the USSR, in taking gratuitously anti-Western positions on non-Balkan questions of great importance to the U.S., and in repressing ruthlessly some of the potentially most anti-Soviet elements in Yugoslavia, are creating a public atmosphere in the U.S. least conducive to American action in support of an imperiled post-Tito leadership. The various peoples composing the Yugoslav state, who have proved their bravery and fierce devotion to independence throughout history, deserve a better fate.

Appendixes

Appendix 1. The Ethnic Heterogeneity of Yugoslavia's Autonomous Republics and Provinces

Key

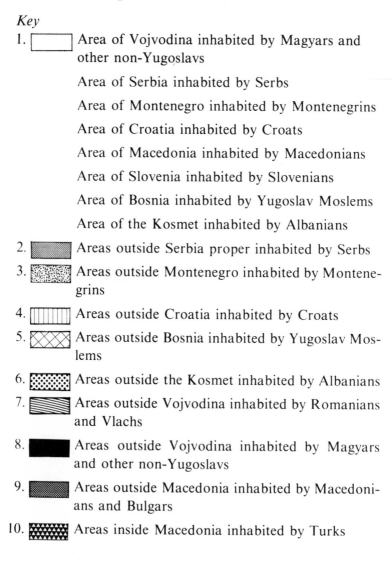

1. Area of Vojvodina inhabited by Magyars and other non-Yugoslavs

   Area of Serbia inhabited by Serbs

   Area of Montenegro inhabited by Montenegrins

   Area of Croatia inhabited by Croats

   Area of Macedonia inhabited by Macedonians

   Area of Slovenia inhabited by Slovenians

   Area of Bosnia inhabited by Yugoslav Moslems

   Area of the Kosmet inhabited by Albanians

2. Areas outside Serbia proper inhabited by Serbs

3. Areas outside Montenegro inhabited by Montenegrins

4. Areas outside Croatia inhabited by Croats

5. Areas outside Bosnia inhabited by Yugoslav Moslems

6. Areas outside the Kosmet inhabited by Albanians

7. Areas outside Vojvodina inhabited by Romanians and Vlachs

8. Areas outside Vojvodina inhabited by Magyars and other non-Yugoslavs

9. Areas outside Macedonia inhabited by Macedonians and Bulgars

10. Areas inside Macedonia inhabited by Turks

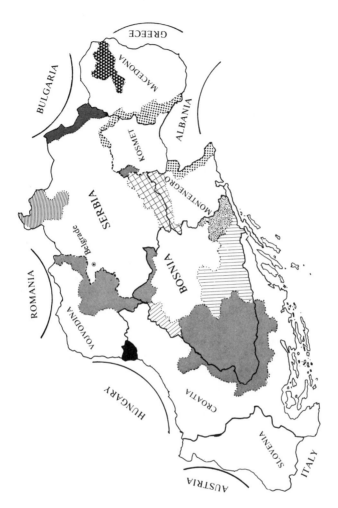

Sources: This original map was extrapolated from maps, charts, and statistics in the following published works: Werner Markert, ed., *Osteuropa-Handbuch: Jugoslawien* (Köln-Graz: Böhlau-Verlag, 1954); Paul Shoup, *Communism and the Yugoslav National Question* (New York: Columbia University Press, 1963); Zdenko Antic, "National Composition of Yugoslavia," RFE 1423, Yugoslavia (May 25, 1972); Slobodan Stankovic, "National Minorities in Yugoslavia," RFE 2001, Yugoslavia (February 21, 1974).

Appendix 2. The Disproportionate Percentage of Croats among the *Gastarbeiter*

Table 1

Total Population and Number
of Workers Temporarily Employed
Abroad, March 1971

Republic	Population		Employed abroad		Percentage share of people employed abroad in total population
	Number (in thousands)	Percentage composition	Number (in thousands)	Percentage composition	
Yugoslavia	20,505	100.0	672	100.0	3.3
Bosnia-Herzegovina	3,743	18.3	137	20.3	3.7
Croatia	4,423	21.6	225	33.5	5.2
Macedonia	1,647	8.0	54	8.0	3.4
Montenegro	530	2.6	8	1.3	1.5
Serbia	8,437	41.1	200	29.8	2.4
Serbia proper	5,242	25.6	115	17.1	2.2
Kosovo	1,245	6.1	24	3.6	1.9
Vojvodina	1,950	9.5	61	9.1	3.2
Slovenia	1,725	8.4	48	7.1	2.9

Source: "Some Basic Features of Yugoslav External Migration," *Yugoslav Survey* 13, February 1972.

Appendix 3. Yugoslavia's Governmental Structure according to the 1974 Constitution

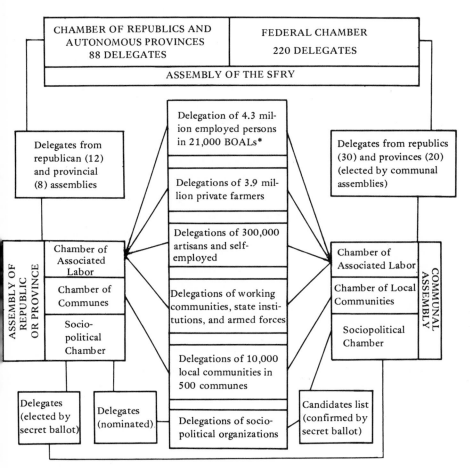

*BOALs (basic organization of associated labor) include enterprises and institutions, local communities, social organizations, the armed forces, private farmers, and artisans.

Source: Slobodan Stankovic, "Yugoslavia's New Electoral System," part 2, RFE 2064, Yugoslavia (May 13, 1974).

Appendix 4. State Treaty for the Reestablishment of an Independent and Democratic Austria (BGBl no. 152/1955)

Article 7: Rights of the Slovene and Croat Minorities

1. Austrian nationals of the Slovene and Croat minorities in Carinthia, Burgenland, and Styria shall enjoy the same rights on equal terms as all other Austrian nationals, including the right to their own organizations, meetings, and press in their own language.

2. They are entitled to elementary instruction in the Slovene or Croat language and to a proportional number of their own secondary schools; in this connection school curricula shall be reviewed and a section of the Inspectorate of Education shall be established for Slovene and Croat schools.

3. In the administrative and judicial districts of Carinthia, Burgenland, and Styria, where there are Slovene, Croat, or mixed populations, the Slovene or Croat language shall be accepted as an official language in addition to German. In such districts topographical terminology and inscriptions shall be in the Slovene or Croat language as well as German.

Source: BGBl no. 152/1955, United Nations Treaty Series, vol. 217, pp. 229-233.

Appendix 5. Topographical Map of Yugoslavia

Source: *Encyclopaedia Britannica Macropaedia*, vol. 19 (Chicago: Encyclopaedia Britannica Inc., 1975): 1101.

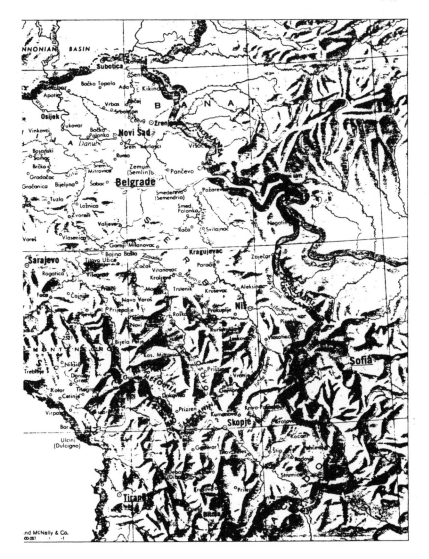

Appendix 6. Greece's Northern Frontier Region

148

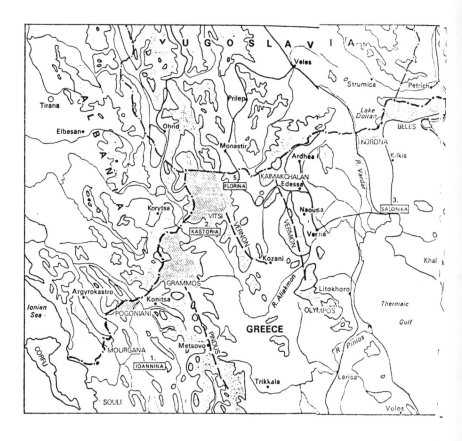

Source: C. M. Woodehouse, *The Struggle for Greece, 1941–1949* (London: Hart-Davis Press, 1976), pp. 224-225.

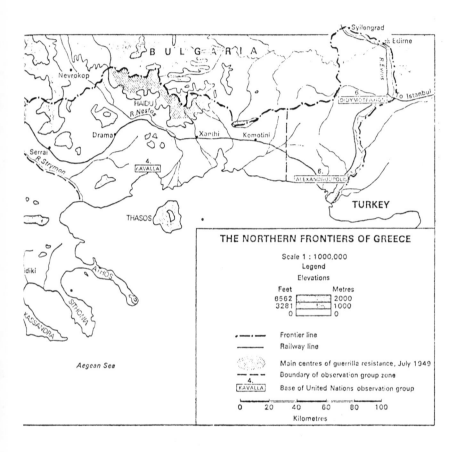

THE NORTHERN FRONTIERS OF GREECE

Scale 1 : 1,000,000
Legend
Elevations

Feet		Metres
6562		2000
3281		1000
0		0

·—·—· Frontier line

——— Railway line

Main centres of guerrilla resistance, July 1949

— — — Boundary of observation group zone

4. KAVALLA Base of United Nations observation group

0   20   40   60   80   100
Kilometres

Appendix 7. The Mediterranean Arena

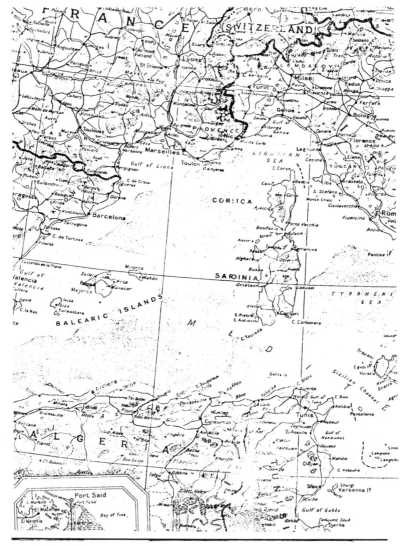

Source: Saul B. Cohen (ed.), *Oxford World Atlas* (New York: Oxford University Press, 1973), p. 22.

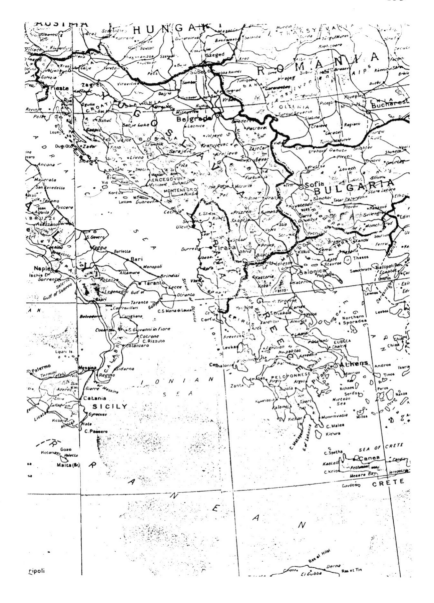

Notes

Notes

Introduction

1. National Democratic Platform, 1976, section on U.S.–USSR Relations, paragraph 3.

2. Paul Shoup, "The National Question in Yugoslavia," *Problems of Communism* 21 (January–February 1972), pp. 18–19.

Chapter 1

1. Slobodan Stankovic, "National Minorities in Yugoslavia," Radio Free Europe Research Papers (hereafter referred to as RFE) 2001, Yugoslavia (February 21, 1974), p. 6.

2. Zdenko Antic, "National Composition of Yugoslavia," RFE 1423, Yugoslavia (May 25, 1972), p. 2.

3. Foreign Area Studies Program of the American University, *Area Handbook for Yugoslavia* (Washington, 1973), p. 40.

4. Stephen E. Palmer, Jr., and Robert R. King, *Yugoslav Communism and the Macedonian Question* (Hamden, Conn., 1971), p. 8.

5. Ibid., p. 7.

6. Included in the "Serbization" program was the denial of the existence of any members of the Bulgarian or Macedonian nationalities in the 1931 Yugoslav census. Census manipulation is a common phenomenon in the Balkans and is dealt with at length in Robert R. King, *Minorities under Communism* (Cambridge, Mass., 1973).

7. King, *Minorities under Communism*, pp. 12–13.

8. Paul Shoup, *Communism and the Yugoslav National Question* (New York, 1968), pp. 52–53.

9. King, *Minorities under Communism*, p. 188.

10. Ibid.

11. Palmer and King, *Yugoslav Communism*, p. 126.

12. Robert R. King, "The Macedonian Question and Bulgarian Relations with Yugoslavia," RFE RAD Background Report 98, Bulgaria (June 6, 1975), p. 6.

13. Palmer and King, *Yugoslav Communism*, pp. 127–129.

14. King, RFE 98, pp. 5–8.

15. Slobodan Stankovic, "New Yugoslav-Bulgarian Squabble over Macedonia," RFE 2016 (March 7, 1974), pp. 1-3.

16. King, RFE 98, p. 9.

17. Palmer and King, *Yugoslav Communism*, p. 14.

18. Ibid, pp. 8–14.

19. Shoup, *Communism and the Yugoslav National Question,* p. 51.

20. Ibid., p. 52.

21. Ibid., pp. 159–165.

22. Ibid., pp. 178–179.

23. Palmer and King, *Yugoslav Communism*, pp. 165–174.

24. Ibid., p. 166.

25. King, RFE 98, pp. 7, 10.

26. Ibid., p. 7.

27. King, *Minorities under Communism*, pp. 189–192.

28. Stankovic, RFE 2001, pp. 6–7.

29. Malcolm W. Browne, "Belgrade Steels Stand on Albania," *New York Times*, November 24, 1975, p. 11.

30. Louis Zanga, "The Meaning of the Latest Demonstrations in Kosovo," RFE RAD Background Report 15 (February 3, 1975), p. 5.

31. Ibid.

32. Ibid., pp. 4–6.

33. Paul Lendvai, "Ferment in the Kosovo," *Financial*

Times (London), March 5, 1975.

34. Current Albanian-Yugoslav relations are the antithesis of those prevailing between Yugoslavia and Bulgaria: local disturbances have prolonged tension on the diplomatic front in the former instance, whereas in the latter case conflicts between the two governments have exacerbated local disharmony. See Browne, "Belgrade Steels Stand," p. 11.

35. Louis Zanga, "Kosovo: An Important Element in Yugoslav-Albanian Rapprochement," RFE RAD Background Report 91, Yugoslavia (June 2, 1975), pp. 1–2.

36. Malcolm W. Browne, "Yugoslavs Appear to Abandon Albanian Rapprochement Bid," *International Herald Tribune*, November 24, 1975.

37. Browne, "Belgrade Steels Stand," p. 11.

38. Dusko Doder, "Yugoslav-Albanian Relations Show Strains," *International Herald Tribune*, March 2, 1976.

39. Peter R. Prifti, *Albania and the Sino-Soviet Rift* (Cambridge, Mass., 1971), p. 17.

40. A. Ross Johnson, *Yugoslavia: In the Twilight of Tito* (Beverly Hills, Calif., 1974), p. 4.

41. Prifti, *Albania and the Sino-Soviet Rift*, p. 19.

42. "Albanian Paper Discusses U.S.–Soviet Relations," Joint Publications Research Service Translations (hereafter referred to as JPRS) 62045, Albania (May 21, 1974), p. 6.

43. "Moscow-Tirana: The Gulf Deepens," *Soviet Analyst* 5, no. 3 (January 29, 1976).

44. Slobodan Stankovic, "Yugoslav Paper Hails Albania's Alleged Changes in Attitude toward Yugoslavia," RFE RAD Background Report 72, Yugoslavia (June 12, 1975), p. 2.

45. Johnson, *Yugoslavia*, p. 36.

46. Slobodan Stankovic, "Bijedic Visits China," RFE RAD Background Report 141, Yugoslavia (October 15, 1975), p. 3.

47. "Concern over Religious Instruction for Albanians," JPRS 65764, Yugoslavia (September 26, 1975), p. 41.

48. Stankovic, RFE 2001, p. 6. .

49. In this connection it may be worth noting that Tito—
who, prior to his 1948 expulsion from the Cominform, operat-
ed on the extreme left wing of the international Communist
movement—apparently enjoyed the support of the Soviet left-
wing Zhdanov-Voznesensky faction, a situation which probably had something to do with the initial choice of Belgrade as
the site of the Cominform's headquarters. The Zhdanov group
seems to have been in the ascendancy in the USSR during this
period, at a time when Stalin appears to have suffered recur-
ring bouts of ill health. In this respect, it is interesting to note
that pictures of the 1946 October revolution anniversary
parade in Moscow reveal not only that Stalin was absent but
also that Zhdanov and his closest Leningrad collaborators
(Voznesensky, Kosygin, and Kuznetsov) monopolized the
center of the dais, to the detriment of Malenkov, Molotov, and
Beria. Presumably, Zhdanov's group became dominant
enough in Moscow to cause its rivals major "loss of face."
Possibly the fall of Tito from the international Communist
leadership, as symbolized by his expulsion and by the transfer
of Cominform headquarters from Belgrade to Bucharest, may
have been related to the gradual demise of the Zhdanov group
in Soviet domestic politics.

50. Details about the history of Albanian-Yugoslav relations are based in part on William E. Griffith, *Albania and the
Sino-Soviet Rift* (Cambridge, Mass., 1963), pp. 12–59. Discussions with Peter Prifti of the Massachusetts Institute of
Technology have been helpful to my thinking on more contemporary aspects of relations between the two regimes. The
history of Sino-Yugoslav relations is based in part on Donald
Zagoria, *The Sino-Soviet Conflict, 1956–1961* (Princeton,
N.J., 1962).

51. Associated Press, "Albanian Leader Planning Less
Material Dependence on Assistance from China," *New York
Times*, November 2, 1976; Reuters, "Belated Greetings Sent to
Peking by Albanians," *New York Times*, October 27, 1976.

52. "Party Chief to Conduct Purge of Albanian Dissidents," *International Herald Tribune*, May 26, 1976.

53. "Moscow-Tirana: The Gulf Deepens."

54. Slobodan Stankovic, "Situation of Hungarian National Minority in Yugoslavia Praised," RFE RAD Background Report 1, Yugoslavia (January 7, 1975), p. 2.

55. Ibid.

56. "Yugoslav Students at Hungarian Medical School," JPRS 65937, Yugoslavia (October 15, 1975), p. 40.

57. Stankovic, RFE 2001, p. 6.

58. MBFR currently is referred to by many analysts as MFR, since the concept of "balanced" reductions, in the view of some observers, has been replaced by a concept of agreement at any price.

59. George Gomori, "Hungarian and Polish Attitudes on Czechoslovakia, 1968," in *The Soviet Invasion of Czechoslovakia: Its Effects on Eastern Europe*, ed. E.J. Czerwinski and Jaroslaw Piekalkiewicz (New York, 1972), pp. 107–119.

60. "Border Dispute with Italy Arouses Yugoslav Press," JPRS 61713, Yugoslavia (April 10, 1974), p. 95.

61. Stankovic, RFE 2001, p. 6.

Chapter 2

1. Slobodan Stankovic, "Yugoslavia—One Year After," RFE 1648, Yugoslavia (December 8, 1972), p. 12.

2. Slobodan Stankovic, "Current Situation in Yugoslavia: An Analysis of Contemporary Ferment," RFE 1266, Yugoslavia (January 17, 1972), p. 9.

3. Malcolm W. Browne, "Yugoslavia Steps Up Drive against Religion," *New York Times*, December 22, 1975, p. 3.

4. Zdenko Antic, "Tension between State and Catholic Church in Yugoslavia Continues," RFE RAD Background Report 112, Yugoslavia (July 1, 1975).

5. Slobodan Stankovic, "Croatian National Assembly to Adopt Own Defense Law," RFE 0838, Yugoslavia (January

21, 1971), p. 1.

6. Ibid., p. 4.

7. Slobodan Stankovic, "On the Problem of Sovereignty for Yugoslavia's Constituent Republics," RFE 1274, Yugoslavia (January 24, 1972), p. 2.

8. "Croat Emigré Paper Attacks Motives of Sejna Interviews," JPRS 61853, Yugoslavia (April 26, 1974), p. 5.

9. Antic, RFE RAD 112, p. 4

10. Josip Jurkovic, "Thirty Years of Crimes—The State Security Service, One of the Main Bulwarks of the Yugoslav Regime," *Hrvatska Revija* (Munich), no. 2 (June, 1974), pp. 239–247; translated in JPRS, July 1974.

11. C.L. Sulzberger, "Most Dangerous Game," *New York Times*, June 9, 1976.

12. Johnson, *Yugoslavia*, p. 41.

13. "West German Paper Reports on Emigré Croat Communist Session," JPRS 61931, Yugoslavia (May 7, 1974), p. 67.

14. Ivan Volgyes, "The Hungarian and Czechoslovak Revolutions: A Comparative Study in Communist Countries," in Czerwinski and Piekalkiewicz, *Soviet Invasion of Czechoslovakia*, pp. 137–138.

15. Sulzberger, "Most Dangerous Game."

16. Stankovic, RFE 2001, p. 6.

17. Shoup, "National Question in Yugoslavia," pp. 20–21.

18. Rankovic led what, in effect, was a coalition of conservative forces (consisting of the parties of the underdeveloped republics and much of the Serbian party) in an attempt to centralize the political system and reverse the liberalization which the country had undergone in the 1950s. To a large degree, when it concerns the question of centralization, the liberal-conservative debate has taken on a definitely ethnic flavor, since the Croatian and Slovenian parties (having been outvoted consistently by the Serbs and their underdeveloped allies) generally have advocated decentralization in favor of wide autonomy for the republics. See Shoup, "National Ques-

tion in Yugoslavia," pp. 19, 21.

19. In 1971, 225,000 workers, or 33.5 percent of the total labor force abroad, had come from Croatia, which contains only 21.6 percent of the population. Moreover, these workers were the most highly skilled and thus, presumably, the highest wage earners among Yugoslavs abroad. See "Some Basic Features of Yugoslav External Migration," *Yugoslav Survey* 13, no. 1 (February 19, 1972).

20. Zdenko Antic, "Tito Intervenes in Croatian Affairs," RFE 1221, Yugoslavia (December 3, 1971), pp. 1–5.

21. Stankovic, RFE 2001, p. 4.

22. Slobodan Stankovic, "Croatian Leaders Attack Centralist Faction," RFE 1985, Yugoslavia (February 7, 1974), p. 2.

23. Stankovic, RFE 2001, p. 5.

24. Malcolm W. Browne, "Yugoslavia Cracks Down on Slovenes Who Urge More Political Freedom," *New York Times*, September 29, 1976.

25. Malcolm W. Browne, "Yugoslav Judge, a Champion of Civil Rights, Is Sentenced to Six Years," *New York Times*, October 16, 1976.

26. Dusko Doder, "Belgrade Suspends Sentence of Lawyer in Dissident Case," *International Herald Tribune*, May 28, 1976.

27. For a transcript of the Mihajlov trial, see the notes taken by Shirley M. Stewart in *The New Leader* 59, no. 2 (January 19, 1976): 7–12.

Chapter 3

1. Slobodan Stankovic, "Praxis Professors Still Survive," RFE 2087, Yugoslavia (July 11, 1974), p. 6.

2. Slobodan Stankovic "Polemics over New Left in Belgrade," RFE 1488, Yugoslavia (July 20, 1972), p. 2.

3. Stankovic, RFE 2087, p. 3.

4. Slobodan Stankovic, "Following the Ouster of Belgrade

Professors," RFE RAD Background Report 14, Yugoslavia (January 31, 1975), p. 1.

5. Stankovic, RFE 2087, p. 4.

6. Slobodan Stankovic, "Yugoslavia: Ideological Ferment at Many Levels," RFE 1984, Yugoslavia (February 6, 1974), p. 3.

7. Slobodan Stankovic, "Belgrade 'Komunist' Attacks 'New Left' in Yugoslavia," RFE 2018, Yugoslavia (March 11, 1974), p. 3.

8. Slobodan Stankovic, "Problems of *Praxis*, the Philosophical Bimonthly," RFE 1356, Yugoslavia (March 28, 1972), p. 2.

9. Slobodan Stankovic, "*Praxis* Editor Attacks Croatian Party Leader," RFE 1971, Yugoslavia (January 22, 1974), p. 1.

10. Stankovic, RFE 1356, p. 3.

11. Slobodan Stankovic, "Growing Student Opposition at Belgrade University," RFE 1953, Yugoslavia (December 27, 1973), p. 1.

Chapter 4

1. Slobodan Stankovic, "Yugoslavia's New Constitution Proclaimed," RFE 2004, Yugoslavia (February 25, 1974), p. 2.

2. Slobodan Stankovic, "Yugoslavia's New Electoral System," part 2, RFE 2064, Yugoslavia (May 12, 1974), pp. 1–7.

3. Stankovic, RFE 2004, p. 3.

4. Slobodan Stankovic, "Yugoslavia's New Electoral System," part 1, RFE 2048, Yugoslavia (April 17, 1974), pp. 2–6.

5. Stankovic, RFE 2064, pp. 3–4.

6. Slobodan Stankovic, "The Role of Yugoslavia's State Presidency," RFE 1924, Yugoslavia (November 22, 1973), pp. 1–2.

7. Ibid.

8. Slobodan Stankovic, "State Presidency: Yugoslavia's Collective State Leadership Gets Standing Rules," part 2, RFE, Yugoslavia (June 27, 1972), pp. 5–6.

9. Zdenko Antic, "Yugoslav Army Influence To Be Strengthened," RFE 2057, Yugoslavia (April 25, 1974), p. 2.

10. Slobodan Stankovic, "Yugoslav Army Party Organization Holds Conference," RFE RAD Background Report 74, vol. 2, no. 14 (April 4, 1977): 1–4.

11. Slobodan Stankovic, "Top Party Hierarchy To Be Reorganized," RFE (RFE-RL) RAD Background Report 108, Yugoslavia (June 6, 1977), pp. 1–4.

12. Slobodan Stankovic, "Party Membership in Yugoslavia," RFE (RFE-RL) RAD Background Report 100, Yugoslavia (May 23, 1976), pp. 1–4.

13. Slobodan Stankovic, "Veselin Djuranovic—Yugoslavia's New Prime Minister," RFE RAD Background Report 58, Yugoslavia, vol. 2, no. 12 (March 21, 1977): 1–4.

14. Slobodan Stankovic, "The Problem of the Succession to Tito," RFE 1791, Yugoslavia (May 11, 1973), p. 3.

Chapter 5

1. "1973 Joint Protocol between Yugoslavia and the USSR," JPRS 65766, Yugoslavia (September 26, 1975), pp. 56–58.

2. Kevin Devlin, "Differences between the Italian and Spanish Communist Parties in Their Attitudes Toward the Soviet Union," RFE RAD Background Report 155, World Communist Movement (November 11, 1975), pp. 1–3.

3. Kevin Devlin, "Yugoslavia, Romania Reaffirm Stand on Warsaw Meeting," RFE 2125, Europe (October 16, 1974), p. 2.

4. "Excerpts from Statements and Speeches of Communist Meeting in East Berlin," *New York Times*, July 1, 1976, p. 12.

5. Ibid.

6. Zdenko Antic, "Increasingly Vigorous Anti-Cominformist Campaign," RFE RAD Background Report 152, Yugoslavia (November 4, 1975), pp. 1–2.

7. Paul Lendvai, "A Stalinist Ghost Walks," *Financial Times* (London), November 7, 1975.

8. Details on the Cominformists, Ustashi, and their conflicts with Yugoslavia and its agencies were compiled from several sources, including interviews conducted in December 1976 with Dr. Ernst Kux of the *Neue Zürcher Zeitung* and in September 1976 with officials of the Bonn Bundeskriminalamt, as well as the following Radio Free Europe reports by Slobodan Stankovic: "Cominformist Trials in Yugoslavia Continue," RFE RAD Background Report 73, Yugoslavia (March 26, 1976); "More on the Cominformist Trials in Yugoslavia," RFE RAD Background Report 39, Yugoslavia (February 1976); and "Tito Sees Yugoslavia's Future Secure, Its 'External Enemies' Attacked," RFE RAD Background Report 124, Yugoslavia (June 2, 1976). See also "Yugoslav Exiles in Belgium Afraid," *New York Times*, August 15, 1976.

9. See *Polizeiliche Kriminalstatistik 1975* (Bundeskriminalamt, Bundesrepublik Deutschland), pp. 40, 45, and appendix pp. 23, 26, 41, 44, 59, 62, 78, 90. KGB and Ustashi activity among Yugoslav *Gastarbeiter* is particularly ominous in view of the fact that some 350,000 of these migrant workers recently have returned to Yugoslavia. Thus "infiltrees" presumably now can operate within Tito's state.

10. David Floyd, "Rebel Communists Reveal Plans To Depose Tito," *Daily Telegraph* (London), February 24, 1976.

11. In connection with the Cominformist threat, as well as other topics, I am indebted to a discussion in August 1976 with Christopher Cviic of the *Economist*, which was most helpful and informative.

12. "West German Paper Reports," JPRS 61931, p. 67.

13. Slobodan Stankovic, "Belgrade Protests against Soviet Support for Anti-Yugoslav Emigrés," RFE 1034, Yugoslavia (June 11, 1971), p. 3.

14. "Great Soviet Encyclopedia Favors Bulgarian Viewpoint on Macedonia," JPRS 61835, Yugoslavia (April 24, 1974).

15. Slobodan Stankovic, "Solzhenitsyn's 'Gulag' to Be

Published in Yugoslavia?," RFE 2006, Yugoslavia (February 27, 1974), p. 1.

16. Kevin Devlin, "Yugoslav Prime Minister Visiting Moscow," RFE RAD Background Report 68, Yugoslavia (April 10, 1975), p. 102.

17. William H. J. Manthorpe, Jr., "The Soviet Navy in 1975," *U.S. Naval Institute Proceedings* 102, naval review issue (May 1976), p. 208.

Chapter 6

1. My analysis of Italian military and political affairs was assisted greatly by discussions with the following persons, in addition to those mentioned in the preface: Anton W. de Porte, policy planning staff, U.S. Department of State; John Stoddart, political adviser to Adm. Stansfield Turner, Headquarters, Allied Forces, Southern Europe, Naples; Walter J. Silva, counselor for political multilateral affairs, U.S. Embassy, Rome; Mr. Wennick, political section, U.S. Embassy, Rome; Brig. Gen. Gaetano Lanfernini, Operations Division, NATO Headquarters, Naples; E. Streetor, deputy chief of the U.S. Mission, NATO Headquarters, Brussels; Col. John Farrar, U.S. representative to the International Military Staff, NATO Headquarters, Brussels; Col. John McKenney, director, Defense Operations Division, NATO Headquarters, Brussels; George Bader, U.S. representative to the Defense Review Committee, NATO Headquarters, Brussels; Comdr. Howard Eldredge (USN), Department of Defense; Richard Burt, International Institute for Strategic Studies, London.

2. Roger E. Kanet, "Czechoslovakia and the Future of Soviet Foreign Policy," in Czerwinski and Piekalkiewicz, *Soviet Invasion of Czechoslovakia*, p. 98.

3. *Corriere de la Serra*, May 10, 1972, p. 1.

4. The territorial dispute, a result of the post–World War II agreements which left most of Venezia-Giulia in Yugoslav hands and de facto partitioned the Trieste area into Italian and

Yugoslav "administrations," appeared to have been settled in Yugoslavia's favor after 1975, when temporary demarcation lines were declared to be final boundaries (in line with the Helsinki "spirit"), depriving Italy of areas (such as Istria, the Dalmatian settlements, and Trieste suburbs) subject to long-term Italian irredentist aspirations. Whatever the legal merits of this settlement, members of the neo-fascist MSI continue to lay claims to these territories. This sentiment is particularly strong in the northeastern sector of Italy, including Trieste itself, where the MSI enjoys relatively strong support. Since supporters of fascism have been known to shift rather easily across the spectrum from right-wing to left-wing extremism (presumably the attraction being extremism in general, rather than a specific ideology), it is not unreasonable to assume that the PCI might attract into its ranks MSI voters and other nationalists if it could claim credit for having regained a part of "Italia Irredenta."

5. Alvin Shuster, "Communism, Italian Style," *New York Times Magazine*, May 9, 1976, pp. 51, 54.

6. Typical of the statements emanating from PCI officials during this period was the well-publicized statement by Berlinguer at the East Berlin conference, which included these declarations: "This meeting of ours is not the meeting of an international Communist body . . . . Ours is a free meeting among autonomous and equal parties, which does not seek to lay down guidelines for, or to bind, any of our parties . . . Each party elaborates autonomously and decides in full independence its own political line, both internal and international . . . .There is and cannot be any leading party or leading state." See "Excerpts," *New York Times*, p. 12.

7. Shuster, "Communism, Italian Style," p. 56.

8. Ibid.

9. Leonid Brezhnev, in a speech entitled "One Year after the Helsinki Conference," reprinted in *Current Digest of the Soviet Press* 28, no. 30 (August 25, 1976): 10.

10. Uri Ra'anan, "Some Political Perspectives concerning the U.S.–Soviet Strategic Balance," in *The Superpowers in a Multi-Nuclear World*, ed. Geoffrey Kemp, Robert Pfaltzgraff, Jr., and Uri Ra'anan (Lexington, Mass., 1974), pp. 18–19.

11. Ibid.

12. There is no reason to doubt that the Soviet leaders, having spent years in the party and in many cases having been educated in party schools, are dedicated Leninists. Probably all of them approach foreign affairs with the same long-term goals in mind. "Only" on tactics do they disagree.

13. Given the Soviet doctrine of inevitable socialist victory, "adventurism" is a terrible error since it threatens to bring about a premature conflict, thereby endangering an otherwise certain victory.

14. Uri Ra'anan, "The USSR and the Middle East: Some Reflections on the Soviet Decision-Making Process," *Orbis* 17, no. 3 (Fall 1973): 953–954.

15. Ibid., p. 955.

16. Radio Liberty Dispatch, February 19, 1969, p. 6.

17. John A. Donoho, "Brezhnev, the Politburo, and the Secretariat of the CPSU—People, Functions, and Trends," Fletcher School of Law and Diplomacy 1973, unpublished, pp. 8, 15.

18. Donoho, "Brezhnev," p. 8.

19. Radio Liberty Dispatch, October 11, 1974.

20. My analysis of the aspects of this topic that pertain to Greece was aided considerably by discussions with the following persons, in addition to those mentioned in the preface: Anton W. de Porte, policy planning staff, U.S. Department of State; John Day, Greek desk, U.S. Department of State; Vladimir Lehovic, political-military affairs officer (NATO–Atlantic), U.S. Department of State; Townsend Freeman, counselor for political affairs, U.S. Embassy, Athens; Dr. A. S. Vlachos, former Greek ambassador to the USSR; Constantine Stavropolous, deputy foreign minister, Greece; G. Vasilatos,

senior member of the Greek Center Union party, former mayor of Athens, and chairman of Parliament; Gen. Menelaos Alexandrakis, former Greek representative to NATO; George Drossos, director of the political section, Greek National Television Network; Odiseo Zulas, correspondent, *Elefteros Cosmos, Elefterotipia*; Petros Angelakis, first political department, second section, Greek Ministry for Foreign Affairs; Evangelos Kofos, director, first political department, Greek Ministry for Foreign Affairs; Peter Thompson, Greek Embassy, London; John Stoddart, political adviser to Adm. Stansfield Turner, Headquarters, Allied Forces, Southern Europe, Naples; Maj. Theodore J. Scotes (USMC), military attaché, U.S. Embassy, Athens; E. Streetor, deputy chief of the U.S. Mission, NATO Headquarters, Brussels; George Bader, U.S. representative to the Defense Review Committee, NATO Headquarters, Brussels; Capt. George Bailey (USN), U.S. delegate to the NATO Military Planning Team; William O'Neil, Office of the Defense Adviser, NATO Headquarters, Brussels; Comdr. Howard Eldredge (USN), U.S. Department of Defense; Richard Perle, legislative aide to Sen. Henry M. Jackson. Valuable ideas were derived also from Edgar O'Ballance, *The Greek Civil War 1944–1949* (New York, 1966) and C. M. Woodehouse, *The Struggle for Greece 1941–1949* (London, 1976).

21. These islands are prohibited by post–World War II agreements from being fortified by the Greeks.

22. Robert G. Wesson, *Soviet Foreign Policy in Perspective* (Georgetown, Ontario, 1969), pp. 75–76.

Chapter 7

1. Stephen Heald, ed., *Documents on International Affairs* (London, 1936), p. 649.

2. *United States/Soviet Military Balance*, Congressional Research Service (Washington, 1976), p. 8.

3. Ibid.

4. Exceptions are made only for submarines being repaired in bases outside the Black Sea, in which case such a vessel must traverse the straits during the daytime and on the surface and must return to its original base, once repaired. Moreover, the Turkish government must be given information concerning the matter. See *Documents on International Affairs*, pp. 653, 654.

5. The convention distinguishes between "capital ships" and "aircraft carriers" in the context of Article 11. For quite some time the Turkish government has accepted the Soviet designation of the 24,500-ton *Moskva*-class vessels as helicopter cruisers rather than as aircraft carriers (*The Military Balance*, 1976–77). While this interpretation may have some validity, since the *Moskva*-class ships carry only Ka-25 helicopters, the recent Turkish decision to allow the new Soviet vessel *Kiev* to traverse the straits makes considerably less sense. Despite Russian contentions that the *Kiev* (and presumably also its sister ships under construction, said to number at least four) is merely an "antisubmarine interceptor" and not an aircraft carrier, it is hard to accept the 40,000-ton vessel as anything but the latter. The ship carries about twenty Yak-36 VSTOL (vertical short takeoff and landing) fighter bombers, whose major assignment seems to be a strike against shore targets in support of amphibious landings. (In addition, the *Kiev* carries more than twenty Ka-25 antisubmarine helicopters.) See John Lawton, "Aircraft Carrier *Kiev* Joins Soviet Mediterranean Fleet," *International Herald Tribune*, July 19, 1976.

6. *Documents on International Affairs*, pp. 659–660.

7. Ferenc A. Váli, *The Turkish Straits and NATO* (Stanford, Calif., 1972), p. 102.

8. *Documents on International Affairs*, pp. 653–654.

9. Váli, *Turkish Straits and NATO*, p. 63.

10. Ibid., p. 111.

11. Ibid., p. 117.

12. In fact, the Soviet navy began to use the two Egyptian ports in a significant manner in 1966, at which time Admiral

Chernobay announced that the Soviet Union intended to maintain a permanent naval presence in the Mediterranean. However, full use of the Alexandria and Port Said facilities did not begin until 1967. See Michael McGwire, et al., eds., *Soviet Naval Policy* (New York, 1975), p. 399.

13. Manthorpe, "Soviet Navy in 1975," p. 208.

14. Avigdor Haselkorn, "The Soviet Collective Security System," *Orbis* 19, no. 1 (Spring 1975): 235.

15. It is a matter of some controversy whether the Soviet *Kynda*-class guided-missile cruisers have onboard reload capacity for their Shaddock missiles. It is possible that all four classes of Soviet guided-missile cruisers are limited to a one-shot capacity, unless provided with bases at which to reload. Furthermore, the Kresta-I also lacks an onboard reload capacity for its Sa-N-1 surface-to-air missiles. See John E. Moore, ed., *Jane's Fighting Ships, 1974–1975* (London, 1974), pp. 74–75, 550–553.

16. United Press International, "Tito Said to Dismiss Recent Soviet Overtures," *New York Times*, December 14, 1976.

17. Váli, *Turkish Straits and NATO*, p. 118.

18. The Soviet aircraft in question presumably would include the MiG-23 Flogger, Tu-28 Fiddler, Yak-28 Brewer, and Yak-28P Firebar multipurpose aircraft, the MiG-25 Foxbat, the Su-15 Flagon-A interceptor, the (aging) Su-7 Fitter-B, the Su-17/20 Fitter-C, the Su-19 Fencer-A strike aircraft, and the (aging) MiG-21 Fishbed. It is rather complicated to establish the ranges of these military planes, since various tradeoffs have to be made between speed, range, and amount of ordnance carried. Thus, under different circumstances, ranges can vary radically. In general, this analysis relies upon what various sources (including *Jane's All the World's Aircraft* and *Aviation and Marine International*) deem to be normal combat radii.

19. This analysis was enriched greatly by discussions held in July 1976 with the then commander in chief of the Allied Forces in Southern Europe (CINCSOUTH), Adm. Stansfield

Turner, and with members of the admiral's staff in Naples. A debt of gratitude is owed to Admiral Turner, who was most gracious in allowing access to personnel and material.

20. *The Military Balance*, p. 9.

21. Norman Polmar, "Thinking about Soviet ASW," *U.S. Naval Institute Proceedings* 102, no. 5 (May 1976): 123.

22. Means Johnston, Jr., "NATO's Southern Region— Problems and Prospects," *U.S. Naval Institute Proceedings* 101, no. 1 (January 1975): 4–9.

23. Alvin J. Cottrell and Wynfred Joshua, "The United States–Soviet Balance in the Mediterranean," in *Brassey's Defense Yearbook* (New York, 1974), p. 95.

Chapter 8

1. My analysis of Yugoslavia's defense posture and capabilities was assisted greatly by discussions with the following persons (in addition to those mentioned in the preface): Paul J. Costolanski, Bureau of Intelligence and Research, U.S. Department of State; Vladimir Lehovic, Political-Military Affairs Office (NATO–Atlantic), U.S. Department of State; William O'Neil, Office of Defense Adviser, NATO Headquarters, Brussels; Col. John Farrar, U.S. Representative to International Military Staff, NATO Headquarters, Brussels; Wing Comdr. Michael Mathews (RAF), former British military attaché, Belgrade; Brig. Gen. Gaetano Lanfernini, former Italian military attché, Belgrade, now in the Operations Division, NATO Headquarters, Naples; Comdr. Howard Eldredge (USN), U.S. Department of Defense; Professor Adam Roberts, London School of Economics; Christopher Cviic, correspondent, London *Economist*; George Drossos, director of the political section, Greek National Television Network; Richard Perle, legislative aide to Sen. Henry M. Jackson.

2. Drew Middleton, "Mediterranean Defenses Worry NATO," *New York Times*, December 28, 1975, p. 2.

3. Ibid.

4. Stankovic, RFE 0838.

5. "New Progress in Yugoslav-Romanian Economic Cooperation," JPRS 63610, International Affairs (December 6, 1974), pp. 1-2.

6. Ibid., p. 2.

7. Slobodan Stankovic, "Macovescu Hails Romanian-Yugoslav Relations," RFE 1931, Yugoslavia (November 30, 1973), p. 1.

8. Robert R. King, "Bulgaria," in *Survey of East European Developments*, RFE RAD Background Report no. 171 (August 5, 1976), pp. 17-18.

9. Christopher Wren, "Brezhnev Arrives on a Visit to Romania to Meet Ceauşescu," *New York Times*, November 23, 1976.

10. *Soviet World Outlook* 1, no. 10 (October 15, 1976): 5-6.

11. Ibid., p. 5.

12. Slobodan Stankovic, "After Brezhnev's Visit to Belgrade," RFE RAD Background Report 236, Yugoslavia (November 19, 1976), p. 2.

13. Malcolm W. Browne, "Yugoslavia and Romania Are Believed to Have Problems with a Project for Joint Production of Jet Fighters," *New York Times*, September 26, 1976.

14. The above statistics on military force levels were compiled from International Institute for Strategic Studies (hereafter called IISS), *The Military Balance 1976-1977* (London, 1976), pp. 12, 23, 30.

15. Zdenko Antic, "National Structure of the Yugoslav Army Leadership," RFE 1373, Yugoslavia (April 12, 1972), p. 3.

16. Slobodan Stankovic, "Yugoslav Party Congress and the Army," RFE 2078, Yugoslavia (June 13, 1973).

17. A good topographical map of Yugoslavia is contained in Werner Markert, ed., *Osteuropa-Handbuch: Jugoslawien* (Köln-Graz, 1954), map 11. (See Appendix 5.)

18. Slavonia, not to be confused with Slovenia, is the

easternmost region of the Croatian republic.

19. William Beecher, "U.S. Arms and Their Role in Yugoslav Defense," *Boston Globe,* March 16, 1976.

20. Malcolm W. Browne, "Richardson Says Yugoslavia Safeguards U.S. Technological Secrets," *New York Times,* November 28, 1976.

21. Dimitrije Šešerinac Gedža, writing in *Borba,* December 7, 1975; translated in *Survival* 18, no. 3 (May/June 1976): 116–117.

22. IISS, *Military Balance, 1976–1977,* p. 30; also see S.W.B. Menaul, "Air Defense of the Homeland," and Bill Gunston, "Army Weapons," in Ray Bonds, ed., *The Soviet War Machine* (London, 1976), pp. 56, 190. During the last decade or so, well over 90 percent of arms transferred to Yugoslavia (estimated to be worth about $600 million in current dollars) have emanated from the USSR and Poland. See U.S. Arms Control and Disarmament Agency (hereafter called USACDA), *World Military Expenditures and Arms Transfers 1966–1975* (Washington, 1976), pp. 76–77.

23. As Adm. Stansfield Turner has pointed out, NATO action essentially requires unanimity of the member states. This factor is likely to slow up any decision of the type that would be required to send aid to an endangered non-NATO state, since hesitation on the part even of the smallest member could prevent implementation of the necessary measures. Thus, rather than NATO action per se, multilateral measures, involving some NATO states or unilateral action by the U.S. might be required to help Yugoslavia.

24. "State Treaty for the Reestablishment of an Independent and Democratic Austria (1955), BGBl. no. 152/1955, United Nations Treaty Series, vol. 217: 229–233.

25. *Aviation and Marine International* 4, no. 9 (September 1976): 45.

26. A discussion with Gen. J. Kuntner of the Austrian Defense Academy on November 4, 1976, was helpful to my

thinking about the Austrian variable in the equation. The conclusions, of course, are my own.

27. Yugoslav Information Center, "Secretariat for Foreign Affairs Protests Treatment of Yugoslav Minorities in Austria," *Yugoslav Facts and News*, no. 93 (October 1974).

28. A representative sample of Carinthian Slovene charges against the Austrian government appears in "Increased Tension in Carinthia Due to Discrimination, Nationalist Activities," JPRS 67822 (August 27, 1976).

29. "Katic Views 'Negativist' Attitude," Belgrade Domestic Service (in Serbo-Croatian), Foreign Broadcast Information Service (hereafter FBIS), December 9, 1974, p. 12; *Ljubljana Delo* (in Slovene), "Cardinal Sin," FBIS, June 19, 1975; Mitja Gorjup, "The Cynicism of a Bad Conscience," *Ljubljana Delo* (in Slovene), FBIS, August 27, 1976.

30. Walter Kreuzer, "Ribcic Comments on Carinthian Minority Issue," *Arbeiter Zeitung*, Vienna (in German), FBIS, September 17, 1975.

31. Gorjup, "Cynicism."

32. Ludwig Marton, "Yugoslav Anti-Austrian Campaign," *Die Presse*, Vienna, August 26, 1976.

33. Anneliese Rohrer, "Dank dafür, dasz sich dieses Kärnten für Österreich bewährt hat," *Die Presse*, Vienna, June 28, 1976.

34. Belgrade *Tanjug* (in English), "Austrian Minority Census Meets Wide Opposition," FBIS, September 27, 1976.

35. Paul Hoffman, "Slovenes in Austria Oppose Census," *New York Times*, November 3, 1976.

36. Wolfgang Oberleitner, "Mini-Minderheiten agitieren nicht," *Die Presse*, Vienna, July 12, 1976.

Chapter 9

1. Shelford Bidwell, "Current Objectives and Soviet Strategy," in *The Soviet War Machine*, ed. Ray Bonds, pp. 42–51. See especially p. 48, map of Soviet ECM and reconnaissance

aircraft routes over Europe.

2. Slobodan Stankovic, "Unacceptable Treatment of Yugoslav Workers in Czechoslovakia," RFE RAD Background Report 161, Yugoslavia (June 16, 1976), p. 4.

3. Dr. Ernst Kux of the *Neue Zürcher Zeitung* discussed this and other significant questions with me in December 1976.

4. Slobodan Stankovic, "Yugoslavia's Difficulties in Using Soviet Credits," RFE RAD Background Report 253, Yugoslavia (December 10, 1976), p. 4.

5. Antic, RFE RAD Background Report 229, p. 6.

6. *Foreign Report (Economist)*, June 23, 1976, p. 5.

7. From an article by M. Loshakov (a member of the collegium of the USSR Ministry of Foreign Trade and head of the ministry's department for trade with European socialist countries) which appeared originally in *Ekonomicheskaya Gazeta*, and was later abridged and reprinted in *Soviet News*, December 9, 1975.

8. This observation is based on discussions with Dr. Kux.

9. Stankovic, RFE RAD Background Report 239, p. 2.

10. "Text of USSR Draft Constitution," Moscow *Pravda*, June 4, 1977, pp. 1–4, in FBIS-SOV-77-109, June 7, 1977, vol. 3, no. 109: 1–28.

11. Slobodan Stankovic, "Belgrade Criticizes New Soviet Constitution," RFE (RFE-RL) RAD Background Report 116, Yugoslavia (June 22, 1977), pp. 1–3.

12. Zdenko Antic, "Yugoslavia," RFE RAD Background Report 171, Eastern Europe (August 5, 1976), pp. 46-51.

13. Zdenko Antic, "Yugoslavia Embarrassed by Dissidents' Activities," RFE RAD Background Report 39, Yugoslavia (February 17, 1977), pp. 1-6.

14. Discussion with Dr. Kux.

15. Ibid.

16. Henry Kamm, "Romanians, While Not Jubilant, Count Gains from Berlin Talks," *New York Times*, July 12, 1976.

17. Belgrade, on the other hand—noting Bucharest's "trim-

ming" in the direction of Moscow—now fears that Ceauşescu may be "selling out." See Malcolm W. Browne, "Ceauşescu and Tito Confer at Retreat," *New York Times*, September 9, 1976.

18. "Yugoslavs Report that Tito Rebuffed Brezhnev on Air and Naval Rights and a Role in the Warsaw Pact," *New York Times*, January 9, 1977. (It is noteworthy that this story carried no dateline, byline, or other indication of its source.)

19. Col.-Gen. Ivan Kukoc interview in Yugoslav newsweekly *Nin*, reprinted in *Survival*, May/June 1977, vol. 20, no. 3: 129.

Chapter 10

1. "Text of 'Declaration' issued by the Headquarters of Croatian National Liberation Forces," *New York Times*, September 12, 1976.

2. An example of such a message was contained in the 1976 National Democratic Platform, in the section on U.S.–USSR relations, Paragraph 3, that stated, in part: "The continued USSR military dominance of many Eastern European countries remains a source of oppression for the peoples of those nations, an oppression we do not accept and to which we are morally opposed. Any attempt by the Soviet Union similarly to dominate other parts of Europe—such as Yugoslavia—would be an action posing a grave threat to peace."

3. "Department of State Summary of Text of Sonnenfeldt Address," *New York Times*, April 6, 1976.

"Finally, on Yugoslavia we and the Western Europeans, indeed, the Eastern Europeans as well, have an interest which *borders on* the vital for us in continuing the independence of Yugoslavia from Soviet domination. *Of course we accept that Yugoslav behavior will continue to be, as it has been in the past, influenced and constrained by Soviet power.* But any shift back by Yugoslavia into the Soviet orbit would represent a *major strategic setback* for the West. So we are *concerned* about what will happen when Tito disappears, and it is *worrying* us a good deal. So our basic policy continues to be that which we have pursued since 1948–1949, keeping Yugoslavia in a position of *substantial* independence from the Soviet Union. Now at the same time we would like them to be less obnoxious, and we should allow them to get away with very little. We should especially disabuse them of any notion that our interest in their *relative* independence is greater than their own and, therefore, they have a free ride" [author's italics].

4. Zdenko Antic, "Yugoslav Comments on Helsinki Anniversary," RFE RAD Background Report 172 (August 6, 1976), p. 3.

5. *Soviet World Outlook* 1, no. 10 (October 15, 1976): 8.

6. Don Oberdorfer, "Kissinger Hits Carter on Issue of Foreign Policy," *Boston Globe*, October 25, 1976.

7. Ibid.

8. Malcolm W. Browne, "Yugoslavia Frees Accused U.S. Spy," *International Herald Tribune*, July 24–25, 1976.

Bibliography

Bibliography

Joint Publications Research translations (JPRS)

"Albanian Paper Discusses U.S.–Soviet Relations." JPRS 62045 (Albania), May 21, 1974.

"Border Dispute with Italy Arouses Yugoslav Press." JPRS 61713 (Yugoslavia), April 10, 1974.

"Concern over Religious Instruction for Albanians." JPRS 65764 (Yugoslavia), September 26, 1975.

"Croat Emigré Paper Attacks Motives of Sejna Interviews." JPRS 61853 (Yugoslavia), April 24, 1974.

"Great Soviet Encyclopedia Favors Bulgarian Viewpoint on Macedonia." JPRS 61835 (Yugoslavia), April 24, 1974.

"Increased Tension in Carinthia Due to Discrimination, Nationalist Activities." JPRS 67822 (Austria), August 27, 1976.

"New Progress in Yugoslav-Romanian Economic Cooperation." JPRS 63610 (international affairs), December 6, 1974.

"1973 Joint Protocol between Yugoslavia and the USSR." JPRS 65766 (Yugoslavia), September 26, 1975.

"Thirty Years of Crimes—The State Security Service, One of the Main Bulwarks of the Yugoslav Regime." Originally published (in Serbo-Croatian) *Hrvatska Revija* (Munich) no. 2, June 1974. JPRS (Yugoslavia), July 1974.

"West German Paper Reports on Emigré Croat Communist Session." JPRS 61931 (Yugoslavia), May 7, 1974.

"Yugoslav Students at Hungarian Medical School." JPRS 65737 (Yugoslavia), October 15, 1975.

Foreign Broadcast Information Service

Belgrade Domestic Service. "Katic Views 'Negativist' Attitude" (in Serbo-Croatian), December 8, 1974. FBIS (Eastern Europe, Yugoslavia), December 9, 1974.

Belgrade *Tanjug* (in English), August 24, 1976. FBIS (Eastern Europe, Yugoslavia), September 27, 1976.

Gorjup, Mitja. "The Cynicism of a Bad Conscience." Originally published (in Slovene) in *Ljubljana Delo*, August 25, 1976. FBIS (Eastern Europe, Yugoslavia), August 27, 1976.

Kreuzer, Walter. "Ribcic Comments on Carinthian Minority Issue." Originally published (in German) in *Arbeiter Zeitung*, September 16, 1975. FBIS (Eastern Europe, Yugoslavia), September 17, 1975.

Ljubljana Delo. "Cardinal Sin" (in Slovene), June 12, 1975. FBIS (Eastern Europe, Yugoslavia), June 19, 1975.

Moscow *Pravda.* "Text of USSR Draft Constitution." June 4, 1977, FBIS (Soviet Union), June 7, 1977.

Radio Free Europe Research Papers (RFE)

Antic, Zdenko. "Increasingly Vigorous Anti-Cominformist Campaign." RAD Background Report 152 (Yugoslavia), November 4, 1975.

_____. "National Composition of Yugoslavia." RFE 1423 (Yugoslavia), May 24, 1972.

_____. "National Structure of the Yugoslav Army Leadership." RFE 1373 (Yugoslavia), April 12, 1972.

_____. "Tension between the State and Catholic Church in Yugoslavia Continues." RAD Background Report 112 (Yugoslavia), July 1, 1975.

_____. "Tito Intervenes in Croatian Affairs." RFE 1221 (Yugoslavia), December 3, 1971.

_____. "Yugoslav Army Influence to be Strengthened." RFE 2057 (Yugoslavia), April 25, 1974.

_____. "Yugoslav Comments on Helsinki Anniversary." RAD Background Report 172, August 6, 1976.

_____. "Yugoslavia." RAD Background Report 171 (survey of East European developments), August 5, 1976.

_____. "Yugoslavia Embarrassed by Dissidents' Activities." RAD Background Report 39 (Yugoslavia), February 17, 1977.

_____. "Yugoslavia on the Way to Economic Recovery." RAD Background Report 229 (Yugoslavia), November 9, 1976.

Devlin, Kevin. "Differences between the Italian and Spanish Communist Parties in Their Attitudes toward the Soviet Union." RAD Background Report 155 (world Communist movement), November 11, 1975.

_____. "Yugoslav Prime Minister Visiting Moscow." RAD Background Report 68 (Yugoslavia), April 10, 1975.

_____. "Yugoslavia, Romania Reaffirm Stand on Warsaw Meetings." RFE 2125 (Europe), October 16, 1974.

King, Robert R. "Bulgaria." RAD Background Report 171 (survey of East European developments), August 5, 1976.

_____. "The Macedonian Question and Bulgarian Relations with Yugoslavia." RAD Background Report 98 (Bulgaria), June 6, 1975.

Stankovic, Slobodan. "After Brezhnev's Visit to Belgrade." RAD Background Report 236 (Yugoslavia), November 19, 1976.

_____. "Belgrade Criticizes New Soviet Constitution." RAD Background Report 116 (Yugoslavia), June 22, 1977.

_____. "Belgrade 'Komunist' Attacks 'New Left' in Yugoslavia." RFE 2018(Yugoslavia), March 11, 1974.

_____. "Belgrade Protests against Soviet Support for Anti-Yugoslav Emigrés." RFE 1034 (Yugoslavia), June 11, 1971.

_____. "Bijedic Visits China." RAD Background Report 141 (Yugoslavia), October 15, 1975.

_____. "Cominformists Trials in Yugoslavia Continue." RAD Background Report 73 (Yugoslavia), March 26, 1976.

_____. "Croatian Leaders Attack Centralist Faction." RFE

1985 (Yugoslavia), February 7, 1974.

―――. "Croatian National Assembly to Adopt Own Defense Law." RFE 0838 (Yugoslavia), January 21, 1971.

―――. "Current Situation in Yugoslavia: An Analysis of Contemporary Ferment." RFE 1266 (Yugoslavia), January 17, 1972.

―――. "Following the Ouster of Belgrade Professors." RAD Background Report 14 (Yugoslavia), January 31, 1975.

―――. "Growing Student Opposition at Belgrade University." RFE 1953 (Yugoslavia), December 27, 1973.

―――. "Macovescu Hails Romanian-Yugoslav Relations." RFE 1931 (Yugoslavia), November 30, 1973.

―――. "More on the Cominformist Trials in Yugoslavia." RAD Background Report 39 (Yugoslavia), February 1976.

――― "National Minorities in Yugoslavia." RFE 2001 (Yugoslavia), February 21, 1974.

―――. "New Yugoslav-Bulgarian Squabble over Macedonia." RFE 2016 (Yugoslavia), March 7, 1974.

―――. "On the Problem of Sovereignty for Yugoslavia's Constituent Republics." RFE 1274 (Yugoslavia), January 24, 1972.

―――. "Party Membership in Yugoslavia." RAD Background Report 100 (Yugoslavia), May 23, 1976.

―――. "Polemics over 'New Left' in Belgrade," RFE 1488 (Yugoslavia), January 22, 1974.

―――. *Praxis* Editor Attacks Croatian Party Leader." RFE 1971 (Yugoslavia), January 22, 1974.

――― *Praxis* Professors Still Survive." RFE 2087 (Yugoslavia), July 11, 1974.

―――. "The Problem of the Succession to Tito." RFE 1791 (Yugoslavia), May 11, 1973.

―――. "Problems of *Praxis*, the Philosophical Bimonthly." RFE 1356 (Yugoslavia), March 28, 1972.

―――. "The Role of Yugoslavia's State Presidency." RFE 1924 (Yugoslavia), November 22, 1973.

———. "Situation of Hungarian National Minority in Yugoslavia Praised." RAD Background Report 1 (Yugoslavia), January 7, 1975.

———. "Solzhenitsyn's 'Gulag' to be Published in Yugoslavia?" RFE 2006 (Yugoslavia), February 27, 1974.

———. "State Presidency: Yugoslavia's Collective State Leadership Gets Standing Rules," part 2. RFE (Yugoslavia), June 27, 1975.

———. "Tito Sees Yugoslavia's Future Secure, Its 'External Enemies' Attacked." RAD Background Report 124 (Yugoslavia), June 2, 1976.

———. "Top Party Hierarchy To Be Reorganized." RAD Background Report 108 (Yugoslavia), June 6, 1977.

———. "Unacceptable Treatment of Yugoslav Workers in Czechoslovakia." RAD Background Report 161 (Yugoslavia), June 16, 1976.

———. "Veselin Djuranovic—Yugoslavia's New Prime Minister." RAD Background Report 58 (Yugoslavia), March 21, 1977.

———. "Yugoslav Army Party Organization Holds Conference." RAD Background Report 74, April 4, 1977.

———. "Yugoslav Paper Hails Albania's Alleged Changes in Attitude toward Yugoslavia." RAD Background Report 72 (Yugoslavia), June 12, 1975.

———. "Yugoslav Party Congress and the Army." RFE 2078 (Yugoslavia), June 13, 1973.

———. "Yugoslavia: Ideological Ferment at Many Levels." RFE 1984 (Yugoslavia), February 6, 1974.

———. "Yugoslavia's Difficulties in Using Soviet Credits." RAD Background Report 253 (Yugoslavia), December 10, 1976.

———. "Yugoslavia's New Constitution Proclaimed." RFE 2004 (Yugoslavia), February 25, 1974.

———. "Yugoslavia's New Electoral System." Part 1, RFE 2048 (Yugoslavia), April 17, 1974; part 2, RFE 2064 (Yugoslavia), May 13, 1974.

————. "Yugoslavia—One Year After." RFE 1648 (Yugoslavia), December 8, 1973.

Zanga, Louis. "Kosovo: An Important Element in Yugoslav-Albanian Rapprochement." RAD Background Report 91 (Yugoslavia), June 2, 1975.

————. "The Meaning of the Latest Demonstrations in Kosovo." RAD Background Report 15, February 3, 1975.

Radio Liberty Dispatches

February 19, 1969.
October 11, 1974.

Books and Chapters in Books

Barker, Elizabeth. *Macedonia: Its Place in Balkan Power Politics*. Hertfordshire, G.B.: Royal Institute of International Affairs, 1950.

Bonds, Ray, ed. *The Soviet War Machine*. London: Salamander Press, 1976.

Christides, Christopher. *The Macedonian Camouflage*. Athens: Hellenic Publishing Co., 1949.

Cottrell, Alvin J., and Joshua, Wynfred. "The United States–Soviet Strategic Balance in the Mediterranean." In *Brassey's Defense Yearbook*. New York: Praeger Publishers, 1974.

Czerwinski, E.J., and Piekalkiewicz, Jaroslaw, eds. *The Soviet Invasion of Czechoslovakia: Its Effect on Eastern Europe*. New York: Praeger Publishers, 1972.

Erickson, John. "Soviet Military Posture." In *Soviet Strategy in Europe*, ed. Richard Pipes. New York: Crane Rusak & Co., 1975.

Griffith, William E. *Albania and the Sino-Soviet Rift*. Cambridge, Mass.: Massachusetts Institute of Technology Press, 1963.

————. *World Power Triangle*. Cambridge, Mass.: Massachusetts Institute of Technology Press, 1975.

Heald, Stephen, ed. *Documents on International Affairs, 1936.* London: Oxford University Press, 1936.

Johnson, A. Ross. *Yugoslavia: In the Twilight of Tito.* The Washington Papers Series, no. 16, Beverly Hills, Calif.: Sage Publications, 1974.

Johnson, Chalmers A. *Peasant Nationalism and Communist Power.* Stanford, Calif.: Stanford University Press, 1962.

King, Robert R. *Minorities under Communism.* Cambridge, Mass.: Harvard University Press, 1973.

Lederer, Ivo J. *Yugoslavia at the Paris Peace Conference.* New Haven and London: Yale University Press, 1963.

Lendvai, Paul. *Eagles in Cobwebs.* New York: Doubleday & Co., 1969.

Macedonicus (pseudonym). *Stalin and the Macedonian Question.* Trans. (from Bulgarian) Christ Anastasoff. St. Louis: Pearlstone Publishing Co., 1948.

Markert Werner, ed. *Osteuropa-Handbuch: Jugoslawien.* Köln-Graz: Böhlau-Verlag, 1954.

McGwire, Michael, et al., eds. *Soviet Naval Policy.* New York: Praeger Publishers, 1975.

McDonald, Gordon C., et al. *Area Handbook for Yugoslavia.* Washington: Foreign Area Studies Program, American University, 1973.

The Military Balance, 1975–1976. London: International Institute for Strategic Studies, 1975.

The Military Balance, 1976–1977. London: International Institute for Strategic Studies, 1976.

Moodie, A.E. *The Italo-Yugoslav Boundary.* London: George Philip & Son, 1949.

Moore, John E., ed. *Jane's Fighting Ships, 1974–1975.* London: Jane's Yearbooks, 1974.

NATO Handbook. Brussels: NATO Information Service, 1976.

O'Ballance, Edgar O. *The Greek Civil War, 1944–1949.* New York: Praeger Press, 1966.

Palmer, Stephen E., Jr., and King, Robert R. *Yugoslav Communism and the Macedonian Question.* Hamden, Conn.: Shoe String Press, 1971.

Polmar, Norman. *Soviet Naval Power.* New York: National Strategy Information Center, 1972.

Ra'anan, Uri. "Some Political Perspectives concerning U.S.–Soviet Strategic Balance." In *The Super Powers in a Multi-Nuclear World,* Geoffrey Kemp, Robert L. Pfalzgraff, Jr., and Uri Ra'anan. Lexington, Mass.: D.C. Heath & Co., 1974.

Remington, Robin A. *The Warsaw Pact.* Cambridge, Mass.: Massachusetts Institute of Technology Press, 1971.

Roskill, Stephen W. "A Strategic Analysis of the Mediterranean." *U.S. Naval Institute Proceedings* 197, no. 819 (May 1971).

Shoup, Paul. *Communism and the Yugoslav National Question.* New York: Columbia University Press, 1968.

Stojkovic, Ljubisa, and Martic, Milos. *National Minorities in Yugoslavia.* Belgrade: Publishing and Editing Enterprises, Jugoslavija, 1952.

U.S. Arms Control and Disarmament Agency. *World Military Expenditures and Arms Transfers, 1966–1975.* Washington: U.S. Government Printing Service, 1976.

U.S. Senate Committee of the Judiciary. *Yugoslav Communism: A Critical Study.* Washington: U.S. Government Printing Service, 1961.

U.S./Soviet Military Balance. Washington: Congressional Research Service, 1976.

Váli, Ferenc A. *The Turkish Straits and NATO.* Stanford, Calif.: Hoover Institution Press, 1972.

Wesson, Robert G. *Soviet Foreign Policy in Perspective.* Georgetown, Ont.: John Wiley and Sons, 1969.

Woodehouse, C. M. *The Struggle for Greece, 1941–1949.* London: Hart Davis Press, 1976.

Zagoria, Donald S. *The Sino-Soviet Conflict, 1956–1961.* Princeton, N.J.: Princeton University Press, 1962.

Magazine Articles and Monographs

Aviation and Marine International 4, no. 9 (September 1976):45.

Bertsch, Gary K. "Currents in Yugoslavia—The Revival of Nationalism." *Problems of Communism* 22, November–December (1973).

Brezhnev, Leonid. "One year after the Helsinki Conference" (speech). *Current Digest of the Soviet Press* 28, no. 30 (August 25, 1976).

Campbell, John C. "Soviet Strategy in the Balkans." *Problems of Communism* 23, no. 4 (July–August 1974).

Donoho, John A. "Brezhnev, the Politburo, and the Secretariat of the CC of the CPSU: People, Functions, and Trends." Unpublished manuscript. Fletcher School of Law and Diplomacy, 1973.

Foreign Report, Economist, June 23, 1976.

Frankel, Josef. "Federalism in Yugoslavia." *American Political Science Review* 49, no. 2 (June 1955).

Gedža, Dimitrije Šešerinac. Article in *Borba*. December 7, 1975. Quoted in *Survival* 18, no. 3 (May–June 1976): 116–117.

Haselkorn, Avigdor. "The Soviet Collective Security System." *Orbis* 19, no. 1 (Spring 1975).

Johnston, Means, Jr. "NATO's Southern Region: Problems and Prospects." *U.S. Naval Institute Proceedings* 101, no. 1 (January 1975).

Jurkovic, Josip. "Thirty Years of Crimes—the State Security Service, One of the Main Bulkwarks of the Yugoslav Regime." *Hrvatska Revija* (Munich), no. 2 (June, 1974). Translated in JPRS, July 1974.

Kukoc, Ivan. Interview in *Nin*. Quoted in *Survival* 20, no. 3 (May–June 1977): 129.

Loshakov, M. Article in *Ekonomicheskaya gazeta*. Reprinted in *Soviet News*, December 9, 1975.

Manthorpe, William H.J., Jr. "The Soviet Navy in 1975." *U.S. Naval Institute Proceedings* 102, no. 5 (May 1976).

1955 State Treaty for the Reestablishment of an Independent and Democratic Austria. BGBl. no. 152, 1955. United Nations Treaty Series, vol. 217, pp. 229–233.

1976 National Democratic Platform. Section on U.S.–USSR Relations, paragraph 3.

Pano, Nicholas C. "The Albanian Cultural Revolution." *Problems of Communism* 23, no. 4 (July–August 1974).

Polizeiliche Kriminalstatistik 1975. Bundeskriminalamt, Bundesrepublik Deutschland.

Polmar, Norman. "Thinking about Soviet ASW." *U.S. Naval Institute Proceedings,* 102, no. 5 (May 1976).

Prifti, Peter R. "Albania and Sino-Soviet Relations." Research project for the Center for International Studies, Massachusetts Institute of Technology, 1971.

––––––. "Albanian Realignment? A Potential By-Product of Soviet Invasion of Czechoslovakia." Research project for the Center for International Studies, Massachusetts Institute of Technology, 1968.

––––––. "Kosovo in Ferment." Research project for the Center for International Studies, Massachusetts Institute of Technology, 1969.

Ra'anan, Uri. "The USSR and the Middle East: Some Reflections on the Soviet Decision-Making Process." *Orbis*, 17, no. 3 (Fall 1973).

Roskill, Stephen W. "A Strategic Analysis of the Mediterranean." *U.S. Naval Institute Proceedings* 197, no. 819 (Naval Review Issue, 1971).

Shoup, Paul. "The National Question in Yugoslavia." *Problems of Communism* 21 (January–February 1972).

"Some Basic Features of Yugoslav External Migration." *Yugoslav Survey* 13, no. 1 (February 19, 1972).

Soviet World Outlook 1, no. 10 (October 15, 1976): 5–6.

Soviet World Outlook 1, no. 12 (December 15, 1976): 5–6.

Stewart, Shirley M. Transcript of trial of Mihajlo Mihajlov. *New Leader* 59, no. 2 (January 19, 1976): 7–12.

Index

Index